So Close,
Yet So Far Apart

So Close, Yet So Far Apart

Stopping *the* Abuse *of* Others

Treasure Life

SYED H. JAFFAR

iUniverse, Inc.
New York Lincoln Shanghai

So Close, Yet So Far Apart
Stopping *the* **Abuse** *of* **Others**

iUniverse, Inc.

For information address:
iUniverse, Inc.
2021 Pine Lake Road, Suite 100
Lincoln, NE 68512
www.iuniverse.com

Buddhism 2548, Christianity 2004, Hinduism 2060,
Judaism 5764, Islam 1424

ISBN: 0-595-32632-3

Printed in the United States of America

For all the
victims of tyranny.

Let's evolve the spirit and power of *just people* into a triumph of human beings who can overcome obstacles to fulfill our dreams of creating a peaceful world.

To my parents,
Jamil Bano and Zainul Abedin

➢ *The greatest discovery of my generation is that a human being can alter his life by altering his attitude.*
—William James

➢ *People deprived of knowledge will lose everything, and those who leave everything to acquire knowledge— through education—will gain everything.*
—Imam Ali b. Abi Talib

Acknowledgements

A very big thank-you to my wife, Raishma, and my children, Rabia, Shahid, Anne, and Shawn for their advice, patience, and love needed throughout the creation of this book. *I love you all.*

And a special thanks to the following two dear friends for their invaluable comments and encouraging words, informing me where I had missed and hit the mark.

Dr. W. Richard Bond and **Anwer A. Zaidi**

---

*If you do not write for publication,
there is little point in writing at all.*
——**George Bernard Shaw**

The Front Cover: It depicts several stars like our solar system has the nucleus (sun) and its major planets in the Milky Way galaxy. The stars on the surface appear to be **so close, yet** they are literally billions of miles apart, like *the abuse of others* calamity on our planet Earth that has made people **so far apart.**

Acknowledgements

Preface

This book, a guide for all human beings, is written with an eye toward *the just people* of the world who may be interested in knowing about the cardinal-eight *simple ways* to handle difficult challenges, such as **the abuse of others**, to make life more meaningful. It discusses the need for a determined and passionate effort with deep conviction to overcome obstacles such as people idiosyncrasies, attitude, illiteracy, poverty, extremism, resistance to change, scandals in high places, destructive religious gurus, and tyrants' hellish actions.

So close, yet so far apart is all about people; it injects powerful, yet simple ideas into your life for evolving a peaceful world and a more peaceful you. The slogan—*we can do it*—has been used to convey the message that it all can be achieved over a long period of time, if we keep trying for long enough and don't give up.

I have tried to set down what I know about the overall needs of our society and our world with a minimum of biases and with a maximum of concrete examples drawn from my own and others' experiences.

My aims are: **stopping the abuse of others;** ending the tyrant superpowers' hellish actions; eradicating illiteracy and poverty; using the strength of alliances among the just to make our book's title *So Close, Yet So far Apart* a thing of the past; and so forth. Putting greater emphasis on doing good deeds toward fellow human beings than on worshipping God <u>and</u> *creating a world without any superficial or unnatural international borders* are the aims that I am hoping we can all subscribe to.

The subject, I am sure people will agree, is timely. The organization of the material is from general to more specific, table of contents is logically organized, and the chapter titles should be attention getting. To get reader's interest from the beginning, I have tried my best to make Introduction, Chapter I, the cover graphics, and several exhibits as attractive as possible to clearly define the benefits of the book. The specificity in noting the areas on which we must concentrate to make a better world and the way all chapters focus on each of these is for the reader's appreciation of the points made.

As a caution, some details in this book, if not taken as constructive criticism for a positive outcome, may seem somewhat provocative. At the outset, however, let me point out that it is an honest attempt to throw light upon the strengths and weaknesses of people, nations, and societies of our world. Also, Chapter—I is somewhat detailed for those who may prefer it that way, anyway; this means some repetition in other chapters.

Finally, the volume is fairly slim, by design, as I have tried to elucidate the important points within it in my own unique way. The next step would naturally be for *the just people* to begin the process of implementing the persuasive arguments offered here with the Strategic Plan for a Triumphant Society's Project *of* the Century. I am hoping that people would want to sign on!

Toronto,   *Syed H. Jaffar*
September 2004

Table *of* Contents

Exhibits

This section contains the following exhibits that should be of interest to all, including the business people.

➤ **Life and People**

Exhibit-A **The *Life* Model**
—<u>Great</u> Human Beings

Exhibit-B **The Human Idiosyncrasies**
—The People Factor

➤ **Strategic Blueprint**

Exhibit-C **Strategic Planning Process**
—The Society

Exhibit-D **Strategic Planning Model**
—Human Beings on Earth

Exhibit-E **The Strategic Plan/Milestones**
—The Triumphant Society

➤ **Business Motivation**

Exhibit-F **Business Motivation-I**
—Future Industry Structure
—The Internet Industry vs. Others
—Most CEOs Burden (I.T.)

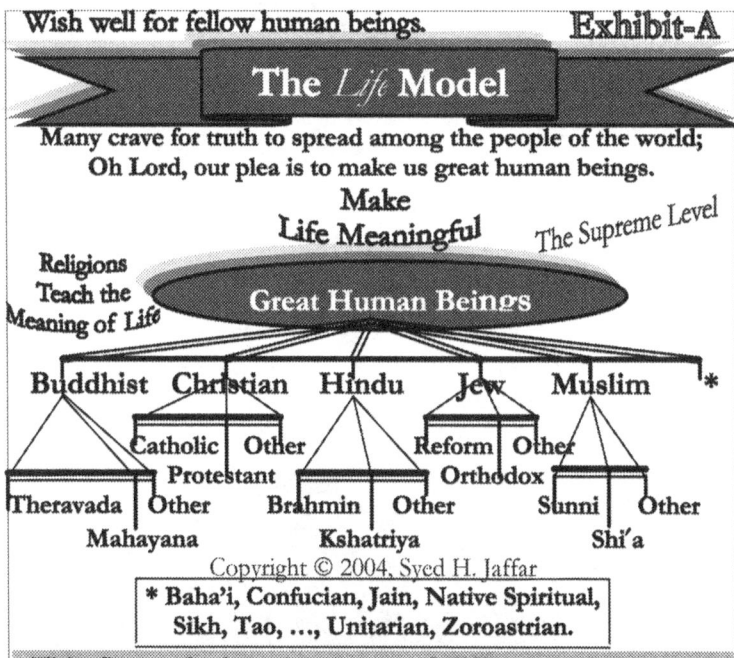

Wish well for fellow human beings.   Exhibit-A

The *Life* Model

Many crave for truth to spread among the people of the world;
Oh Lord, our plea is to make us great human beings.

Make
Life Meaningful   The Supreme Level

Religions
Teach the
Meaning of Life   Great Human Beings

Buddhist   Christian   Hindu   Jew   Muslim   *

Catholic   Other   Reform   Other
Protestant   Orthodox
Theravada   Other   Brahmin   Other   Sunni   Other
Mahayana   Kshatriya   Shi'a

Copyright © 2004, Syed H. Jaffar

* Baha'i, Confucian, Jain, Native Spiritual,
Sikh, Tao, ..., Unitarian, Zoroastrian.

This figure depicts the camps of different religions and their respective pillars, or religious sects. For different religions and cultures, religions are here to stay to teach the meaning of life. To *make life meaningful*, we have to earn the right to be called Great Human Beings, evolving a peaceful world by using the *simple ways to handle difficult challenges* such as human idiosyncrasies, illiteracy, poverty, and the *abuse of others* calamity. As well, to gain inner and lasting peace, we have to begin a glorious journey toward developing a passion for people by putting *greater emphasis on doing good deeds toward fellow human beings than on worshipping God.*

Having truly earned these essential ingredients for success, the love we feel for people, the respect we have for different religions and cultures, and the level of compassion we have for our own religion's uniqueness will increase dramatically to treasure life.

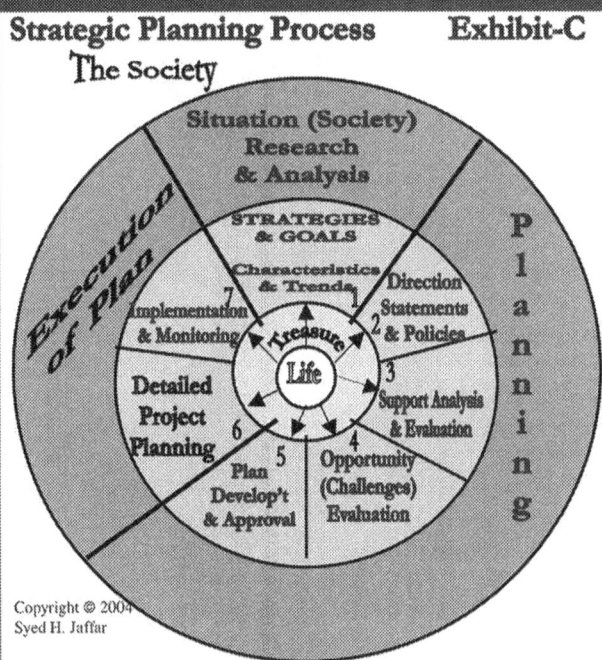

Strategic Planning Process   Exhibit-C
The Society

Copyright © 2004
Syed H. Jaffar

The Strategic Planning Process illustrated here depicts a circular figure to emphasize that planning is a continuous, clockwise process of sequentially inter-related steps. It must look not only at the tools but also at the situation (society) that is being supported and the people and processes that will make it happen.

It is a process whereby the teams of key people do the following:

- Identify the strengths, weaknesses, opportunities (challenges), and threats to a given situation (society).
- Determine the most effective strategies for the situation (society).
- Create an action plan designed to implement the chosen strategies.

Strategic Planning Model
Human Beings on Earth
Exhibit-D

ENVIRONMENT (SOCIETY)
Home, Gov't., Corporate, Economy, Socio-Demography,
Knowledge-Education/Science/Technology

Political, Social,
Cultural, Religious

MAJOR SEGMENTS

* CHALLENGE: Root Cause of
the WRONGs.

MIND -Open/Closed
ATTITUDE -Good/Bad   OUTPUT
EXPECTATION -Realistic/Unrealistic
VISION/VALUE -Constructive/Destructive
RIGHT/WRONG* MIX

Individual, Group, Just-People,
Great Human Being, Society,
Tyrant, Madman...Warlord,
Bad Religious Guru

COMPLEX DEMOGRAPHY

Men
Women   INPUT
Children
Old Folks
SIMPLE DEMOGRAPHY

DIFFICULT CHALLENGES Problems/Opportunities	SIMPLE WAYS to Handle Difficult Challenges
Root Causes. Attitude. Human-Idiosyncracy. Poverty & Illiteracy. Extremism & Criticism. Abuses (Power/People/Sexual/Name-of-Religion/Legal/Health/Welfare). Discrimination. Inequality.... Tyrant, Madman, Warlord, and Superpower-Lord's Hellish Actions. Religious Gurus' Destructive Views.	Change Attitude-People-Systems-Life. Stop Abuses, Extremism/Criticism, & Tyrants/Gurus' Hellish Actions. Provide Models for Right vs Wrong. Create a World without Borders. Educate to Eradicate Illiteracy/Poverty. Eliminate Scandals in High Places. Spread Truth.... Use Common Sense, Just-People Power & Peaceful Means.

THE STRATEGIC PLAN /Milestones
The Triumphant Society

Exhibit-E

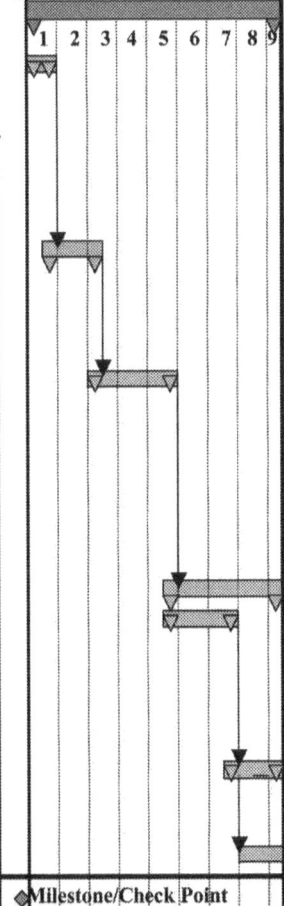

TRIUMPHANT SOCIETY's PROJECT *of* the CENTURY	By	Timeline in Decades								
		1	2	3	4	5	6	7	8	9
1. THE INFRASTRUCTURE										
▪ **Chief Executive (Sponsor)**										
▪ **Active Steering Committee**										
▪ **Full Time Project Manager**										
▪ **Dedicated Project Team**										
▪ **Project Team Home**										
▪ **Project Tools/Technology**										
2. RESEARCH & ANALYSIS										
▪ **Strategies, Goals & Scope**										
▪ **Characteristics & Trends**										
▪ **Scope Review**										
3. THE PLANNING										
▪ **Direction Statements**										
▪ **Policies & Procedures**										
▪ **Support Analysis**										
▪ **Evaluation/<u>Contin</u>gency**										
▪ **Opportunity Evaluation**										
▪ **Design/Development Plan**										
▪ **Plan's Approvals**										
4. EXECUTION *of* PLAN										
4.1 DETAILED PROJECT										
▪ **Design/Development**										
▪ **Testing**										
▪ **Training**										
▪ **Scope/<u>Contin</u>. Review**										
▪ **Go/No-Go Decision**										
4.2 IMPLEMENTATION										
▪ **Pilot—a Region**										
▪ **Rollout—the World**										
4.3 MONITORING/SUPPORT										

◆ Milestone/Check Point

Business Motivation-I   Exhibit-F

Future Industry Structure
2005–2010   —Source: *Microsoft*

➤ **Super Stores** 7x24 e.g., Walmart 700 in 5 Years; $165B to $650B
➤ **Super League:** Krogers, Quixtar, Safeway, Walmart, Webvan

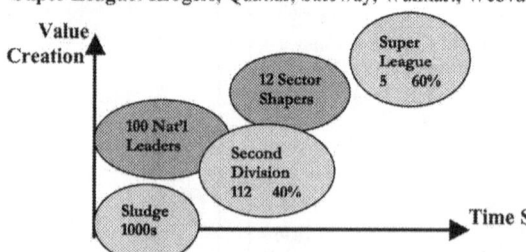

The Internet Industry vs. Others
A Virtual Internet in the Sky by 2020
For the World and Beyond

➤ **"Shopping on the Internet: Up 300% (1997-1998)…**
   Sr. Executives on the Move," Peter Jennings, ABC News
➤ **Discount Stores $290Billion, Franchises $803B**
          …**The Internet: $5Trillion in 2001**
➤ **AOL.com**   **$64Billion**   vs.   **GM $53Billion**
➤ **Yahoo.com**   **$37.5B**   vs.   **CBS $24.5B**
➤ **Amazon.com**   **$22.5B**   vs.   **Sears $19B**
➤ **Priceline.com**   **$??.?B**   >   **RJR Nabisco,..**

Most CEOs Burden (IT-Information Technology)
-CEOs may not like IT, but they can't live without it.

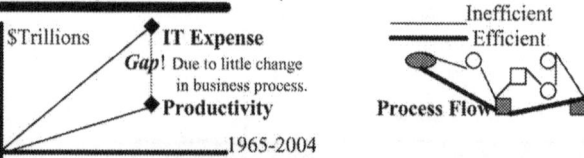

Business Motivation-II Exhibit-G

Plan *for* Extraordinary Changes

➤ **Excel in All Three Dimensions of Management to Dominate Market.** *–Harvard Business Review*
  -Score 10 out of 10 in each.
  -Falling short in any means struggling to survive.

Quality (Better)

Time (Faster)

Cost (Cheaper)

➤ **More Effectively Manage the Organization**
  -Survive the dramatic changes
  -Take advantage of **e**-commerce

➤ **Look Five Years Out (Ask Questions)**
  -In what products or service markets would we participate?
  -Who will be our customers? How will we reach them?
  -Who will be the competitors?…our competitive advantage?
  -Where would our margins come from?
  -What capabilities will make us unique?

Adopt New Attitudes

➤ **Accept drastic changes or the winds of change.**
➤ **Improve the business processes.**
➤ **Make decisions and transform business into e-biz.**
➤ **Provide enterprise-wide solutions.**
  -All key players to participate and see the big picture.
➤ **Make personal commitment to customer service (smile).**
➤ **Quality: Exceed customer expectations and continually improving the business process.**
➤ **Ready-Fire-Aim-Fire (Experience), *Not* Ready-Aim-Aim-Aim from here to eternity (Stop analyzing).**
➤ **Put customers at the top of your organization chart. Believe in your organization's vision and values.**
➤ **Use foresight not just forecasting.**
➤ **Achieve excellence as a way of life to take your organization into a new and promising era.**

Business Motivation-III   Exhibit-H

The Quest for Survival

➢ "The future just ain't what it used to be."—**Yogi Berra**
➢ "Business as usual" is now **Business as *unusual*.**

Proactive

Digital Transformation

Reengineering

Continuous Improvement

Restructuring

Reactive   **Downsizing**

**Rethink the Business Model.
Not just improve, but
possibly replace.**

Short Term   **Long Term**

➢ "You can wait to begin the implementation while you think
through your strategy. What you can't wait any longer to do is the
planning and education process."
—**Jack Shaw**, Author of Surviving the Digital Jungle.

Digital Transformation Timeline   —Jack Shaw

Enterprise-wide e-Biz Strategy

Process Transformation Priorities
(Mission Critical Business Processes)

E

D   **3 Years**

C

B   **2 Years**

A   **1 Year**
Smallest/Easiest   **Core Technological**   **People Skills**
for an Easy Win   **Capability (Corp. Asset)**   **Infra Structure**

Digital Transformation Policies & Procedures

Time

➢ **The choice is not whether, but how to do it.**
-Customer Demands and Competition Threats.

➢ By being proactive, we can provide more value, reduce costs, improve quality &
productivity, and gain the long-term competitive and strategic advantage.

The Science of Politics and Religion

Excerpts from this book, published in the U.S.A., 2004
By Kirk Winstune, An American Writer and Author.

Exhibit-I

Global Political Systems   —Kirk Winstune

As we review the many countries and nations around the world, we come to understand that much of the geo-political make up is based on religious beliefs and divisions. Likewise, much of the war and violence in the world is founded on religious beliefs and divisions. The Middle East is a hotbed of hate and violence. *[As are the political and religious conflicts particularly in: Palestine, the Middle East (Jews vs. Christians and Muslims): Kashmir, the East (Muslims vs. Hindus); Northern Ireland, the West (Catholics vs. Protestants); and the U.S.A., the "9/11" September 11, 2001 attacks.]*

Historically, religion has played at least as great a role in geo-politics. Most conquest was done in the name of the god and religion of the conquering army. The Christians invading the Holy Lands during the crusades and the Catholics invading the empires of Mexico and South America, to relieve them of their—pagan ways and gold. *[The Jews and the Romans brutally crucifying Jesus Christ. The Muslims expanding from Spain through North Africa to Indonesia and from Russia to Southern Africa. The Hindus in India capturing Goa (Christians), Hyderabad (Muslims), and Kashmir (Muslims).]* Millions of lives were ended and destroyed in these and similar conquests. The Catholic Church tortured and murdered many of its members during the Inquisition, as great an institutional slaughter as any socialist regime has committed.

The Science of Politics and Religion

Excerpts from this book, published in the U.S.A., 2004
By Kirk Winstune, An American writer and author.

Exhibit-J

Religious Truth   —Kirk Winstune

What is religious truth then? Religious truth is never found in ancient tales of animal spirit incarnations, or magical dogmas or incantations, or propaganda enforcing allegiance to the institution. It is never found in the chanting of the names of gods and goddesses or of incessantly repeated verses of religious beliefs. Religious truth is just truth.

How can humans know what truth is? They must follow clear, uncluttered patterns of discovery that lead to understanding the true nature of things. It is the same process as any other path of inquiry.

Before we can eliminate wars and contentions, and countless other human divisions, which invariably lead to suffering and a general stifling of the human condition, we must eliminate the false beliefs of humanity. Each person must learn to think independently of any institution. Before people align themselves with any group or collection of people with similar beliefs and goals, it should be only after a logical, reasoned, and balanced inquiry into the matter. This is the only method that can prevent the kind of enslavement and abuse that is common throughout the world.

Introduction

Many crave for truth to spread among the people of the world.
Oh Lord, our plea is to make us great human beings.
—The *Life* Model

We know political leaders, religious groups, social and cultural segments, corporate sectors, and other people are under a lot of pressure these days to do something about today's deadliest conflicts, immense atrocities, merciless abuse of others, and the endless human sufferings around the world. Destruction, bloodshed, misery, and suppression have been caused both by past and present tyrants' lust of power and their desire to make people go, as credible books point out, "tremendously astray."

Yes, the truths about militarily powerful tyrant political leaders, warlords, dictators, madmen, and bad religious gurus with destructive views, as well as other problems or challenges, such as human idiosyncrasies or the "people factor" (see Exhibit-B), illiteracy, poverty, and abuse of the name of religion are real. Either the root causes of these problems are being ignored, or there is seemingly no real effort to get to the bottom of it all. The trigger-happy super powerful leaders, or "boys playing with their big toys," at best, appear to be touching the surface as temporary solutions to these problems.

If we were to go on operating in this blind, militaristic mode of asserting supremacy, the serious problems of hatred with violent retaliation, human suffering, and the decay of human dignity will worsen many fold and, therefore, will continue to be among our most difficult challenges. As will be the *abuse of others* calamity that, in essence, has prompted me to write about all peoples of our world as *so close, yet so far apart.*

To make this title of our book as a thing of the past, it is imperative that we closely identify, prioritize, and get to the root causes of all the ills and problems of the world, first. Then and only then, we passionately try to solve one problem at a time with high level of determination and deep, almost obsessive, conviction over a long period of time. We must, therefore, seriously regard what Confucius—a Chinese philosopher in the sixth century BCE—said, *"It cannot be, when the root is neglected, that what should spring from it will be well ordered."* Ignoring that, I am afraid, human suffering will continue to be the biggest challenge among other misfortunes of the world.

The truths about human suffering and the adversities around the world have been substantiated throughout this book. At the outset, however, for better appreciation of the gravest degree of these tragedies, let's examine the poetic work of the nineteenth century ultimate maestro and an architect of the Urdu language from the Indian Subcontinent—Mir B. A. Anis.

The wound that no balm can heal,
The pain which none but the heart does feel;
The burn that ever rends, The grief that never ends;
The sorrow that severs body and soul,
Is the loss of {human beings and human dignity} to a
suff'ring soul!

—Translated by Dr. S N A Rizvi

Despite all that doom and gloom, there is hope because people who believe in right versus wrong and just cause can overcome obstacles to fulfill our dreams of evolving a peaceful world. With perseverance and a high level of determination to succeed in achieving this noble cause, the strength or power of alliances among the just *can do it* if they keep trying for long enough and don't give up.

Another relatively simpler and faster approach as a start for our goal of achieving peace would be to persuade the smaller or weaker nations—in terms of "gunpowder" and particularly those in the Middle East—to skillfully, tactfully, and genuinely try and make peace with the super powerful nations. I strongly recommend it with some certainties that it will work against those who may be planning to destroy them.

The super powerful nations—their current leaders' large effigies have been trampled upon and burnt by millions of just people protesting and peacefully marching against the evils of tyranny in the major cities of the world, including London and New York City—are also under pressure from their own people to avoid unnecessary wars that kill their young men and women in the thousands. They realize that these wars fuel the situation many-fold and leave their soldiers increasingly isolated and lonely to the point that some of them even commit suicide. I, therefore, urge both parties to reach out and give this strategy a try; both of them will have little to lose and probably a lot to gain.

My real heroes are those super-powerful leaders and others who go for a win-win strategy to win peace not wars. This ***win-win*** strategic move will make those individuals, groups, or nations—that are currently on the road for destroying or abusing others—melt and, sooner than later, will have to join the peace move as well. Hence, the beginning of a glorious journey toward our ultimate goal of achieving peace on Earth.

Given today's political or religious conflicts around the world, this may seem as an impossible proposition. However, what may seem impossible today may not be so in the future—the near future.

In support of this strategy, here are some examples. Try and think of the nations that were allies and those at war against each other during World War II last century. Soon after World War II, the Soviet Union became a staunch enemy of its former allies during the cold war era. As well, Japan and Germany that were at war with the rest of the world during World War II are now on the same friendly world boat as the rest of us.

The other two more recent examples that I can give here in support of my proposed strategic move are, first, today's tactful and genuine approximation of Libya and Pakistan. Libya has not only decided but actually has been actively doing something about it in the recent past to show the world that it really means peace with all nations; many European countries are genuinely welcoming this move.

Pakistan also wisely chose to cooperate and work with the superpowers at the peak of a serious international crisis after "9/11" September 11, 2001 attacks on the United States of America. Pakistan decided to become a significant ally when Afghanistan was over-run by some local Afghan ground forces with an overwhelming U.S. air support. At the initial stages, however, the U.S. war strategy included pushing buttons to direct missiles to locations in Afghanistan from the distant and safe areas in the Arabian Sea.

The final example, that is very relevant to the current Middle East situation, is the historic diplomatic attempt in 1977 by Egypt's President Anwar Sadat who very sincerely took the initiative to make peace with Israel that truly had welcomed it from the very top—true heroism from both sides. Once again, *my definition of true heroism is to win peace not wars.* Deplorably though, Sadat was assassinated by a home grown fundamentalist assassin in Cairo, Egypt on October 6, 1981, and that, unfortunately, was the beginning of the end of the heroic peace initiative.

Assuming we can understand the veracity of human sufferings, discrimination, and inequality, and then *accept and respect* the principle of **different realities** (defined later) in the twenty-first century, we just might begin a glorious journey toward developing a passion for people, peace, and tranquility.

Better yet, *putting greater emphasis on doing good deeds toward fellow human beings than on worshipping God* might be the key to earning the supreme level of great human beings to make *life* meaningful. Hence, we will gain inner and lasting peace for our ultimate goal of treasuring life.

Another key for controlling the dimensions of the future, at least for the followers of three major religions, is *Abraham* (Avraham in Judaism and Ibrahim in Islam), the Model of Sacrifice, who lived about 2000 BCE and stands out as the shared ancestor of Jews, Christians, and Muslims. *Abraham*, as Bruce Feiler—an American author of best seller book, *Abraham*—writes, "holds the key to our possible reconciliation…we can relate it to contemporary religious and political conflicts."

As well, the entire world population of over six billion people today should learn from the past great examples of the magnificent seven Models of Life and Models for Right vs. Wrong.

The seven grand religious, spiritual, and political Models of Life are: Moses of the Land of Israel, The Buddha of the Himalayas (NE India), Jesus Christ of Nazareth, and Imam Hussain b. Ali—grandson of Prophet Mohammed of Mecca-Medina, Arabia. To continue, Mahatma Gandhi of the Indian Subcontinent, Mao Tse Tung of China, and finally John F. Kennedy of the United States of America. Some information on these grand figures can be found in Chapters—I and details in Chapter—III.

As for the principle of **different realities** referred to earlier, it states that the differences among individuals are every bit as vast as the differences among many cultures and religions around the world, the mother *of* all realities. "It's not a matter of merely tolerating differences," as Dr. Richard Carlson—an American lecturer and famous best-selling author of Don't Sweat the Small Stuff…and it's all small stuff—points out, "but of truly understanding and honoring the fact that it literally can't be any other way."

When we learn how to accept and respect the reality of vast differences among individuals, cultures, and religions, our life won't be perfect, but we will learn to accept and respect what life, cultures, and religions have to offer with far less resistance. According to China's Zen Buddhism philosophy, when we learn to *let go* of problems instead of resisting with all our might, our life will begin to flow.

It may sound trite or over used to stress the need to know the *meaning of life* through a religion and where it's taking us, but sound understanding has to reflect a religion's *raison d'etre* (that which has justified its existence) and our belief in it. The connection between a religion's vision and values that *teach the meaning of life* <u>to</u> great human beings that *make life meaningful* may not always seem straightforward.

Nevertheless, understanding the impact on people and every religion's golden rule—to *wish well for fellow human beings*—can help make those links clearer. The actual wording of one religion's golden rule, for example, is *"Not one of you truly believes until you wish for others what you wish for yourself."*

There is profound similarity in each major religion's own wording of this golden rule. This highly significant resemblance in the golden rules together with our shared ancestor—*Abraham*—should make us *so close,* yet, because people have been mercilessly abusing other people, we have become *so far apart*.

This, in essence, is the real issue that prompted me to come up with *The Life Model* (see Exhibit-A) that pleads: *Many crave for truth to spread among the people of the world. Oh Lord, our plea is to make us great human beings.*

In this unique book, I will share with people the details of some very powerful, yet **simple ways** that we can begin to work on now, to gracefully survive and strive in this world. We'll find that the cardinal-eight *simple ways* will apply to some very **difficult challenges** (detailed in Chapter I) that we will face in our quest for evolving a peaceful world over several decades.

The simple, yet powerful and non-violent means, as well as the long-term approach (see Exhibit-E The Strategic Plan/Milestones—The Triumphant Society's Project of the Century) presented in this book, as opposed to instantaneous solutions or false expectations of overnight revolutions, are what make this book unique.

As well, the volume of this book (or handbook) is somewhat slim, by design, for the people to hopefully read it anywhere, even when traveling. Better still, as you implement the ideas outlined here into your life, I assure you that you will begin to evolve a peaceful world and a more peaceful you.

The cardinal-eight **simple ways**, nevertheless, will involve good communication at all stages throughout this mammoth effort over generations with *clear goals and milestones* as to what gets done by whom and when? It will also take a look at the bigger picture. An effective long-term process will reflect the culture of our people, the way they will interact effectively, and the values that they will share worldwide.

The following list contains the cardinal-eight **simple ways** as detailed (what, how, and by whom) in Chapter I: 1. Change, Change, Change (—Attitude, People, Systems, and Life,—Tyrant Superpowers' Hellish Actions). 2. Stop the Abuse of Others (—Use the Strength of the Just). It will mean stopping the superpower-lords from creating a man-made hell on earth.

Superpower-lords in this book are defined as dictators, madmen, people with the "mad-cowboy" disease, tyrant political leaders, warlords, bad religious gurus—mullahs, priests, and pundits—with extreme or destructive views, and, generally, the *people and power* abusers.

Continuing with the *simple ways*: 3. Provide a Model for Right vs. Wrong. 4. Facilitate Education for Eradicating Illiteracy and Poverty. 5. Check Extremism and Criticism. 6. Create a World without Borders. 7. Eliminate Scandals in High Places. 8. Use Common Sense.

As well, make a determined effort to become The Life Model (see Exhibit-A), to accept and respect different people, religions, and cultures—the mother of all realities. The exhibit depicts the camps of different religions that teach the meaning of life. To make life meaningful, however, we have to earn the supreme level of great human beings by respecting all religions and yet appreciating the uniqueness of your own religion.

If I were to pick one key simple strategy here at this introduction stage, then that would have to be Change Attitude. Reading through this book, you'll see yourself that attitude is a major problem. We must change our tune and quick. Always remember that *"I"* and *"mine"* attitudes don't equate with inner peace. Changing your own attitude, undoubtedly, will be the key when trying to change other people and in the process changing your own life.

Furthermore, to be a strong and powerful nation in non-military terms for a long time (centuries), it is imperative that countries with wealth, jewels, and money change their attitude as well. Hoarding wealth (e.g., the old Spain) and banking an "infinite" amount of money (e.g., today's Saudi Arabia) in their own or foreign banks are not the answers. What they really need is to heavily invest in developing something like the industrial revolution of Britain of the nineteenth century.

It's a dangerous world with uncertainty, a world of a few madmen. These *so few* madmen or tyrants have been abusing *so many*. The *so many*, however, must use the strength of *just people power*, the biggest power of all, to make determined efforts with nonviolent and peaceful means to free this world from the disease of those very few tyrants. The most recent and great example of using ***people power*** would have to be the hundreds of thousands of Ukrainian people peacefully rallying for several days in the freezing temperatures of Kiev against the outcome of disputed or "rigged" Ukrainian presidential elections in November 2004. As I put my very final finishing touches to this book, I hear that they have won their demands, as the country's parliament in an emergency session declared the election results invalid and, soon, illegal. Should or could all this have happened in Florida, meaning the U.S. elections of year 2000?

Despite significant achievements, particularly by women, in trying to eliminate *discrimination and inequality* in our society, it's still very much a man's world today. The people who believe in right and just cause will have to do a lot more than they have done to date to create a world with equality, little discrimination and, yes, lots of fairness.

Furthermore, we have to check the abuses in our health and welfare systems, and change our legal system where people are getting away with murder if they can afford to hire a really good lawyer. Lawyers, incidentally, also write the laws of the land in a language only they can understand. Now, that to me is like asking inmates to write the rules of prison systems. We will have to change all that and annul the retirement age of 65. Above all, let's persuade or even force the lawmakers to *abolish the death penalty* because it's inhumane and barbaric; it is still practiced in sixty-six countries around the world today. Working together as a cohesive team, *we can do it.*

To continue our quest for evolving a better and peaceful world, we must begin to work together as a strong and cohesive team to form more powerful coalitions and organizations around the world. Needless to say, we are not talking about organizations, such as the current powerless United Nations, where veto power is used almost on any issue, making them as some say the useless or ineffective groups. Their resolutions (e.g., on Kashmir and the Middle East) that survive the veto power are often no more than just a piece of paper that gets filed away in the archives.

In my humble effort here, we are talking about the proposed organizations where people come together as equals and have the power to act together, in order that they can achieve their right and just goals. At the end of the day, it is the **just people power,** not the nuclear power, nor is it the veto power that will change the world for a better and peaceful place for all.

One way to achieve these just goals, perhaps, would be to ask the *so fe*w tyrants to imagine themselves at their own funeral. It will allow the tyrants to look back at their life while they still have the chance to make some important changes. They will probably, as someone once wrote, get a wake-up call that can be an excellent source of change. Hence, they can be made to provide service and good deeds toward fellow human beings.

As for the rest of us good folks, we are also to provide service and good deeds toward fellow human beings without telling anyone about it or expecting anything back in return, because, when we do, we always notice a beautiful feeling of ease and inner peace. Mahatma Gandhi, the greatest spiritual influence, once said, "Love is not love which asks for a return."

Finally, all corporations are to focus on their people. These people are their real strength. They have to value these people and maintain a genuine interest in each employee as a human being with feelings. Proper tools and training, overall quality, and practicing the principle of excellence in customer service are the keys if they want to survive in this competitive world. This means meeting and exceeding the customer expectations, as well as continually improving the business process. For business motivation, it is strongly recommended that people from the corporate sector pay attention to the guidelines offered in Exhibits-F, -G, and -H.

Well, having prepared ourselves for the big challenges, let's now briefly look at some **difficult challenges** (detailed in Chapter I) that we will have to handle with commitment, dedication, and a high level of determination to succeed in evolving a peaceful world.

First are human idiosyncrasies or the people factor (see Exhibit-B), which are the most difficult factors to handle. Second are poverty and illiteracy that are the root causes of all troubles and problems in the world today. Third are the *people and power* abuses by madmen, religious gurus with extreme and destructive views, and tyrants, yes, the superpower-lords who are perhaps being used as pawns by those with wealth and wrong influence to achieve their ulterior motives.

Lastly are abuse of the name of religion with many bloody confrontations and conflicts among four of the world's major religions—Christianity, Hinduism, Islam, and Judaism. For example, the decades old continuing struggles in the Middle East (Jews vs. Christians and Muslims), Jammu and Kashmir in the Himalayas of the East (Hindus vs. Muslims), and Northern Ireland (Catholics vs. Protestants) in the West.

Another example is the "9/11" or September 11, 2001 attacks on the United States of America's World Trade Center—WTC twin towers in New York City—and on a portion of the Pentagon in Washington, D.C. The details on the 9/11 attacks and the above mentioned other three major conflicts can be found in Chapter I.

As a final note on challenges, some very powerful nations in the recent past decades have managed to create a few **little monsters** (e.g., Saddam Hussein of Iraq) in some regions of the world to serve their purpose. These little monsters, however, after years of subserviently committing atrocities in their own and neighboring countries (e.g. Iraq's war with Iran for a decade), turned against their masters, who eventually have had to destroy them with hardly any challenge.

The much bigger challenge to face, worth noting, would be when these powerful nations have to one day face the big monsters they have created, to preserve their own military and nuclear supremacy.

If the trend of the supremacy mode of the past centuries were to continue <u>and</u> the foreign destructive influences in this country don't succeed, then all indicators today point toward the truly hard working, well disciplined, and united one billion strong people of China to be the next real superpower. It was Napoleon Bonaparte who said, "Let China sleep, for when she awakes she will shake the world." Also, the former U.S. President, Bill Clinton recently said that fate of the world hangs on how China defines its greatness.

China's strength or its future power, worth noting, would not be gained by copying the cunning diplomacy, the gunpowder power, or military supremacy of the powerful old Western Europe, the former Soviet Union (now Russia), or the United States of America—U.S.A.

Instead, China would develop into a strong, united, and highly disciplined people-power combined with an unprecedented industrial revolution that will surpass the nineteenth century British mark and the current automobile and electronics industry of Japan. Japan, as we know, has managed to capture the world, meaning the world market, including Europe, the Americas, and all, through the superior quality, durability, and performance of its products.

The foundation for a strong, independent, and self-sufficient China in every category (nuclear and space race to sports—simply look at the results of 2004 Summer Olympics—and everything in between) was laid by Chairman Mao Tse Tung in the twentieth century.

As I finish writing these paragraphs, I hear in the news that China has just surpassed Canada as number-one U.S. trading partner. This probably is just the beginning of more such and bigger successes ahead for China. Incidentally, my brother, an American from Boston, Massachusetts, as a senior executive engineer was among the American pioneers who set up businesses in China for American businesses in the 1970s–1980s.

As for the present day U.S., it, like its wild Texas style western movies and with its military supremacy, tells the world to behave and do exactly what it expects or else...die. Let me draw a perfect analogy or give an example here. In an old western movie, a cowboy on his horse slowly passing through a village shoots and kills an Indian boy who was just sitting, looking, and minding his own business. The reason given, when asked by his companion cowboy for the shooting, was that the boy didn't smile at him.

The powerful Soviet Union, in the last century, enjoyed its adventures by putting a grip on the Eastern European countries, and Western Europe, which has had all six continents of the world under its grip, had relished its preponderancy during the past few centuries.

Western European atrocities, supremacy, and hold included *desolation* of the local original population of the Americas, Australia, New Zealand, and apartheid or racial segregation in Africa; as well as grabbing the wealth and precious stones or jewels, even from the pillars and walls of some wealthy countries like India.

For example, the 5,000 years old Koh-i-Noor (meaning "mountain of light") from the original 240 to now a more brilliant 108.93 carat diamond—mounted on over 2,500 other diamonds—of the Mogul Emperors from the Indian Subcontinent made its way to England in 1850 for Queen Victoria. It's originally from the Indian Subcontinent but through different conquerors it traveled to Iran, Afghanistan and then back to India. It's now a grand part of the British Imperial State Crown. A year earlier, Mogul Emperors' Timur Ruby had found the way to Queen Victoria as well; it's now part of the necklace worn by Elizabeth II on state occasions. India has put a claim to these precious stones but nothing has come of this claim as yet.

Thomas Paine, an eighteenth century famous American writer, as someone wrote, passionately argued for independence from Britain and the ability of the young country, the U.S.A., to prosper unfettered by the oppressive and economically draining English.

North America, worth noting, was a heaven for the potato-starved or famine-stricken Irish people and for the bubonic-plague-suffering population of the British Isles in the seventeenth century. Australia was used for the British convicts who were deported there, and Asia and Africa were victimized through some cunning diplomacy, deceiving business practices, and of course the gunpowder.

Invasions of Mexico and South America by the Spanish and Portuguese Catholics, a couple of centuries in the past, were mainly due to religion and the motivation to grab gold but partly were inspired by the great voyages of two well-known European explorers. The first was Christopher Columbus, a navigator from Genoa, Italy, who sailed toward the West and discovered the Americas. The second was Vasco da Gama, a Portuguese navigator, who circled the Cape of Good Hope a couple of times and then finally sailed to India. Both of these discoveries took place in the late fifteenth century CE.

The powerful era of the old Western Europe (Portugal, Spain, France,...the Netherlands, and Britain) and the current, peaking in effectiveness, U.S. military power or dominance are no different to some other powers or dynasties that had their "hay days" before it.

For example, the Christians invaded the Holy Lands during the crusades; the Catholic Church tortured and murdered many of its members during the Inquisition, as great an institutional slaughter; and the Jews and the Romans brutally crucified Jesus Christ. As well, the Muslim or Islamic expansion and harsh domination for many centuries that had covered a vast area from Spain through North Africa and India to Indonesia, and from Russia to Southern Africa. Finally and more recently, the Hindus of India who over ran Kashmir, Hyderabad, the Sikhs' Golden Temple in Amritsar, and the Christian Goa. Oh, what a human mess; I almost feel like asking Adam, the father of the human race, to start all over again.

Nevertheless, by applying a twenty-twenty vision with a positive attitude and with some realistic goals to accomplish the **simple ways** for survival, we, the just people using the strength of alliances, can face the above mentioned difficult challenges using nonviolent and peaceful means.

We should use foresight and not just forecasting for making drastic changes. Forecasting projects tomorrow based on what is today. Foresight, on the other hand, identifies tomorrow and determines the interim process or strategy. We'll have to make the transition because halfway measures will mean failure. We will also need a high level of determination and dedication to succeed, to evolve our world into a better and peaceful place for all.

A lasting peace will virtually eliminate human suffering and current huge military expenditure. This will not only mean saving lives but enormous savings in monetary terms. Then, by utilizing a fraction of these financial savings, we can fight other wars such as reducing *political and religious tensions, illiteracy, and poverty* on Earth.

Our expectations will have to be at a realistic level too. As you can imagine, peace on Earth is not something we will achieve overnight, perhaps, not even in our lifetime. It may be several decades or a century before we get there, by then with all new people. Nevertheless, we must begin and make certain that our struggle to achieve our goal of evolving a peaceful and just world will continue into the next generations as well.

Because once we have truly accomplished some or all the cardinal-eight **simple ways** for survival, the love we feel for the people, the respect we have for other religions and cultures, and the level of compassion we have for our own religion's uniqueness will increase dramatically. Hence, we will gain inner and lasting peace for our ultimate goal of treasuring life.

Finally, in an effort to demonstrate my credibility and to build trust with my readers, let me share a few words about my background and experiences that I will always treasure. For over three decades, I have had the pleasure of working as an Information Technology—IT professional with medium to large organizations of the United Kingdom's and with North American (Canada, the U.S.A., and the Caribbean) major and diverse industries. My earlier working experiences were in Pakistan and with the then world's largest oil company (Arabian-American) in Saudi Arabia.

Having been associated with the I.T. field for so long, some people, who try to be kind, call me one of the pioneers of the modern IT—information technology. Well, I wouldn't be too sure about the pioneer bit. What I am very sure about, however, is that I am not someone like Microsoft's Bill Gates—not by any imagination—who is known as an I.T.

"whiz kid" and is now one of the richest men on Earth, if not the richest man.

In 1999, Bill Gates also wrote a New York Times' best seller, Business @ The Speed of Thought. In it, he wrote: If the 1980s were about quality and the 1990s were about reengineering, then the 2000s will be about velocity;...a digital nervous system will let you do business at the speed of thought—the key to success in the twenty-first century.

Gates, as I am led to believe, has also made his company, Microsoft, *paperless* but that for the rest of us realistically speaking should translate as significantly *less paper*, at least for a while longer. As should we translate the automation *with no human interaction* to automation with some *face-to-face* reality as an absolute key to success for any business.

Other keys to business success, based on my own experiences (see Exhibit-E, phase-1 of The Strategic Plan/Milestones—Triumphant Society's Project of the Century), are: First, acquiring the *CEO's sponsorship and support* throughout the life cycle of an I.T. project or any other project of strategic magnitude. Second, forming an executive steering committee of senior executives headed by the CEO to monitor the progress of the project, to assign priorities, and to resolve any conflicts that will always be there as a fact of life.

Third, making one person (project manager) accountable for the successful completion of the big and long-term assignment, a "superman" who is technically adequate but more importantly is business oriented and possesses exceptional people and communication skills. This person must also be a good listener, a leader and mentor, a team builder, and someone who can and is more than willing to take the responsibility of being someone who is *on the book to deliver*.

Fourth, selecting *a dedicated team of knowledgeable* key people from each business unit, key business partners—e.g. customers and suppliers, well-trained technology gurus with competency in the state-of-the-art technology, and business systems analysts and data base administrators who are more business oriented. The project team must be provided a home and is adequately equipped with the tools and technology that will be needed to get the job done.

Fifth and last, for a competitive advantage, *streamline business processes* to boost productivity and efficiency that result in higher revenue, profit, and market share, before embarking on any technical or I.T. solutions. Failing in any one of these *five pillars* of or five key essential ingredients for success, the I.T. false promises in the past forty years of *decreased costs and increased productivity* will continue.

The Year 2000 compliance conundrum was a pressing issue for the business community during the final whole decade of the last century, but contributed little or nothing toward increased productivity. These challenges add to the burden most CEOs carry today—they may not like IT, but they can't live without it (see Exhibit-F).

Finally, and above all, ensure that an *I.T. department directly reports to the CEO or to the highest position* in an organization. Information Technology in the twenty-first century is not the computers or adding machines of the 1950s and, therefore, should not be accountable to the second level e.g., Accounting or Finance area. Some frustrated I.T. people call this area, the bean counters area that gears toward more like a bookkeeping effort to record and control expenses than toward investment or creative accounting.

Today's I.T. department in many medium to large organizations has become the strategic partner of all business strategies, the unparalleled changes, and in providing feasible and optimum technology and business solutions to make an organization the supplier of choice (service or product). Working together with the business partners, I.T. will continue to help organizations to survive and strive in the twenty-first century's digital jungle or information age.

Finally, to end the discussion on my experiences, all those years have meant working very closely with all kinds of people (e.g., clients, customers, senior executives and other co-workers, business partners such as vendors, government agencies, etc.), with my family, relatives, friends, and yes, bridge, cricket, and tennis players. In the process, we helped ourselves to approach work and life in a more pleasant and accepting manner.

We worked mostly with the good people but also with a few that were not so good. Among the not so good, who with destructive or non-cooperative attitude were hindrance toward progress with bad influence on the morale of the rest of the team, were simply removed. This step, fortunately or unfortunately, was taken only on an exceptional basis as the last resort.

Working together as cohesive teams, however, we managed to cultivate productive relationship in dealing with all types of issues or challenges—human or people idiosyncrasies, change, motivation, frustrations, stress, productivity, efficiency, and multi-million dollar projects of strategic magnitude. I also endeavor to achieve excellence, not so much to win rewards but as a way of life. In the process, however, I have indeed won awards of excellence.

As a freelance writer and guest columnist for a leading national weekly publication in Canada, one of my articles, "*Next-gen IT Managers Need to Change Attitudes,*" received rave reviews. Recently, representing myself without the help of any lawyer, I (Appellant) won a significant court case, worth thousands of dollars to me, against Her Majesty the Queen (Respondent) who was represented by a professional counsel in a Canadian court of law.

I earned the designation of Information Systems Professional—ISP *of* Canada, and acquired my degree in Administrative Studies (Business Administration and Computer Science) from Toronto's York University's evening program, the hard way.

Speaking of the hard way, writing something such as what I have written here is hard work for me. To get it published is even harder; it certainly is far too long a process. However, it all was a worthwhile effort and very meaningful.

Much more meaningful than that in the final analysis are: *putting greater emphasis on doing good deeds toward fellow human beings than on worshipping God;* believing in our shared ancestor—*Abraham*, and raising our self-esteem to much greater heights. These essential ingredients undoubtedly will have to be the keys to *make life more meaningful.*

To gain *inner and lasting peace,* each person must learn to think independently of any religious institution—see Exhibit-J Religious Truth, and stop the war and violence based on religious and political divisions—see Exhibit-I Global Political Systems. Above all, we must learn from the magnificent seven religious, spiritual, and political grand

Models of Life and Models for Right vs. Wrong (see details in Chapters I and III).

When all the aforementioned essential ingredients for success in creating a peaceful world have been attained in the true sense, let's hope and pray that our book's title *So Close, Yet So Far Apart—Stopping the Abuse of Others* will become the thing of the past—Amen.

Treasure Life

___:___:___:___

I.

So Close,
Yet So Far Apart

Stopping *the* Abuse *of* Others

(A Long Summary)

Many crave for truth to spread among the people of the world.
Oh Lord, our plea is to make us great human beings.
—The *Life* Model

Humankind has come a long way from the Dark Ages and the Agricultural Era through the Industrial Revolution of the nineteenth century and twentieth century's automobile and airplane inventions to the Digital E-Commerce jungle or Information Age of the twenty-first century. Will the next epoch be a Life or Humanity Evolution? That's a "million-dollar" question among other questions, as the twenty-first century with the third millennium arrives here.

What changes are in store for us? Will we still need the political systems or religions, as we know them today? Can the **just people** make the tyrants and other *people and power* abusers a thing of the past? Will the religions get along? Will the Day of Judgment be part of this century or millennium? What sorts of challenges await us as we struggle to satisfy the internal and external demands of our existence on Earth? The answers to these questions about the future, obviously, cannot be very reliable. The future role of today's political, cultural, social, and religious world, specifically the people-made differences, is very blurry.

What is not blurry, however, is the one common or basically similar rule of all major religions that primarily says *wish well for fellow human beings.* Another common determinant in all this is a man called *Abraham* (Avraham in Judaism and Ibrahim in Islam), a Model of Sacrifice from about 2000 BCE, who stands out as the shared ancestor of Jews, Christians, and Muslims.

This shared ancestry in *Abraham* <u>and</u> the profound similarity in each major religion's basic rule should make us *so close, yet* we are *so far apart* due to *so few* tyrants and madmen that have *mercilessly* been abusing *so many* people. It has made people lose touch with the magic, beauty, and the real meaning of life and religions that have been passed on to us by the magnificent seven Models of Life.

These grand religious, spiritual, and political Models of Life are: Moses of the Land of Israel; The Buddha and a prince of a petty Kingdom of the Himalayas—NE India;

Jesus Christ of Nazareth; Imam Hussain b. Ali, grandson of Prophet Mohammed of Mecca-Medina, Arabia. As well, Mahatma Gandhi from the Indian Subcontinent; Mao Tse Tung of China; and John F. Kennedy of the United States of America. A few brief notes on the life of these magnificent seven, as I call them, can be found later in this chapter followed by some details in Chapter III.

However, our survival as human beings depends on a twenty-twenty vision and how quickly we adopt some new attitudes. Changing your own attitude will be the key when trying to change other people and in the process change your own life. The greatest discovery of my generation, as the early twentieth century American psychologist and philosopher William James said, is that a human being can alter his life by altering his attitude.

We need to move toward accomplishing the cardinal-eight **simple ways** to handling difficult challenges, developing a passion for the people, and raising the level of determination to succeed in creating a peaceful world. Yes, to achieve this mammoth goal, we will have to face the difficult challenges such as human or people idiosyncrasies, illiteracy, and poverty, as well as tyrants, madmen, others abusing so many people, and large groups of misleading people who are abusing the name of religion.

Using military force (gunpowder, bombs and atomic bombs, and other however more sophisticated war arsenals) is too easy and certainly ineffective an approach for handling these challenges or problems. It barely touches the surface of the problems and, therefore, is a temporary solution only. If an overall goal is to eliminate these problems, then we must identify them more closely first and then try to get to the root causes of them all.

A systematic approach to get to the root causes is to investigate as comprehensively as possible covering all areas with clear sequence of events and background of the problems, as well as a team with clear mind and little bias or prejudice. The key to success in applying this approach would be the universally accepted chief executive, I call a constructive "Godfather", whose sponsorship and support— and that of a worthy successor—would be a must throughout the process of trying to achieve our goal of evolving a peaceful world.

As for critical self-examination, we have to start taking everything we do personally. In our determination to succeed in accomplishing the **simple ways** to handle **difficult challenges** (the *simple ways* and *challenges* are detailed later in this chapter), we must make a personal commitment to achieving excellence in everything we do. We should realize that a good effort is not going to be good enough in the twenty-first century; only excellence (not perfection, because that should be avoided) will be acceptable as good enough. We have no alternative.

Before getting into the cardinal-eight **simple ways** (what, how, and by whom) for survival, let's now have a brief look at Realistic Goals, Great Human Beings, The Challenges, and Peaceful Means.

Realistic Goals

To accomplish the **simple ways**, we have to have the wisdom to distinguish between unrealistic and realistic goals. For example, it would be unrealistic to expect accomplishing the *simple ways* for creating a peaceful world overnight or even in our lifetime. To be realistic, it will be a long-term struggle over several decades or even a century to get there when there will be all new people. Also, it would be unrealistic to expect people to practice all religions or to convert all of us to one religion. It's simply not very practical, nor is it possible.

Besides, most people will put up roadblocks mainly due to the fact that practically all of us are totally conditioned by identified social structures from the day we are born. It is almost impossible to even minutely change our way of life and our blind faith without an extraordinarily purposeful and goal directed plan.

Closer to reality, as I see it, is the *acceptance and respect* of the principle of *different realities*, specifically different people, religions, and cultures—the mother *of* all realities. We should realize that the people-made differences among religions are every bit as extensive as the differences among many cultures around the world. As Dr. Richard Carlson wrote, "it is not a matter of merely tolerating the differences but of truly understanding and honoring the fact that it literally can't be any other way."

Great Human Beings (The Supreme Level)

It's refreshing to hear visionaries state their belief that we are not Catholics and not Protestants but we are Christians. Similarly, it is good to listen to scholars and visionaries like Dr. Kalbe Sadiq say that we are not Sunnis and not Shi'as but we are Muslims. Unfortunately, though, these visionaries have stopped short of explicitly mentioning *the supreme level*—great human beings to make life meaningful, as depicted in *The Life Model* (see Exhibit-A). The Model urges people to spread the truth around the world, as well as it pleads for us to become great human beings.

Imagine, just for a moment, that you are not a Buddhist, Christian, Hindu, Jew, or Muslim, but instead would like to become a great human being to make life meaningful. If and when we do achieve or earn that supreme level, it will naturally make us accept and respect the reality of *different people, religions, and cultures—the mother of all realities,* and raise the level of compassion we have for our own religion's uniqueness. We will need it all to move toward developing a passion for people, and to gain *inner and lasting peace* for our ultimate goal of *treasuring life.*

I have seen an understanding of some of it change my two older children's lives. Both, incidentally, have double degrees each with honors from the University of Toronto. I am very proud of the fact that we (yours truly and my first wife—a good human being from beautiful Switzerland; she and I shared life for over twenty most memorable years) never forced any religion upon them. They were never discouraged either about getting to know or practicing the good things of any religions of their own choice.

I would be more than satisfied if this is the one and only good thing I have done in my life. They may not be perfect, but they appear to be reasonably happy people as not forcing any religion upon them has virtually eliminated religious prejudices, quarrels, and destructive criticism (also see Exhibit-J Religious Truth). Our two younger children, interesting to note, at my second wife's wish are being brought up to follow her religious beliefs with an emphasis on the great human being aspect of it all.

A note worth mentioning, we tried to enroll our young son in a Catholic school but that was disallowed because neither of his parents is a Catholic. This was not a "win-win" but was a "lose-lose" situation, because we couldn't get our above average son into an above average school. As for the two systems, I believe that having a Public as well as a Catholic school system are fine. However, if we want to better utilize the public funds, I suggest that they do away with the *duplication* of School Boards' state-of-the-art buildings and most of the administration staff; yet still be able to administer and provide good education to our young human beings.

As young or not so young great human beings, we do believe in providing service and good deeds without telling anyone about it or expecting anything back in return because, when we do, we always notice a beautiful feeling of ease and inner peace. Mahatma Gandhi, the greatest spiritual influence, once said, "Love is not love which asks for a return." As well, *forgive* people and forget. Mother Teresa, one of the world's greatest humanitarians wrote in a poem, *"People are often unreliable, illogical, and self centered; forgive them anyway."* Enjoy reading the full poem at the end of Chapter III.

For business motivation to survive and strive in the twenty-first century, all corporations are to use the guidelines offered on Future Industry Structure, Extraordinary Changes, New Attitudes, and The Quest for Survival, in Exhibits-F, -G, and -H respectively. Remember that the "business as usual" has now been replaced with the reality of *"business as unusual."* The business executives must also focus on their people (employees, customers, and vendors) the subject of this book. Their people are their real strength. Maintain a genuine interest in each employee as a human being with feelings. Truly value your staff and take time to be close to them. This will earn their loyalty, anyway.

The other important entity they have to focus on is their consumer. They have to be "C" Centric—customer, client, and consumer. Also, they must know how to effectively use the "P" Power—planning, projection, product, price, promo, profit, partner, people, place, and productivity.

It is imperative that the front line staff or employees, the only group that is in touch with the customers day in and day out—others are too far removed from the customers' reality, are well **trained** and do practice the principle of excellence in customer service and overall quality. As well, make sure that employees understand and believe in your company's vision and values.

Also, anticipate the customer, client, or user needs and think beyond basic customer satisfaction. Always listen to and learn from a customer's complaints. Researchers have pointed out that one person who complains represents another 200 customers who do not. *The ones who don't complain never come back.* Remember to always include a few key customers or consumers, vendors, and employees in your planning and show respect for their concerns. We also have to change our notion of overall quality. This means meeting and exceeding the customer expectations and continually improving the business process.

We won't need consultants, studies, proposals, meetings, and more meetings on the subject. Also, don't wait for the useless and ineffective annual performance appraisals to record something that happened months before, tell them as and when it's really important enough to do so.

Simply ensure that the front line people provide customer service with a smile, a genuine smile, that comes only from a happy employee; this means using a pull, not push, management methodology. As well, the best approach will entail genuinely linking management and all with the customer or consumer at the top of a hierarchical organization chart. Get a hint from a specific part of the world—Japan— where a customer is referred to by some as God.

As a final note, companies will have to do away with the hierarchical structure of any organization charts. Instead, they should use something similar to a round table structure, but more importantly, where everyone in his or her own area of responsibility, especially the front line staff and workers, feel just as important as anyone else in the organization.

For those who want to keep the vertical and horizontal structure, I suggest that a maximum of "six by six" structure for a medium to large organization is the way to run the business. For example: CEO or president, vice presidents, directors, managers, supervisors, and line workers—the most important entity. Any direct reporting must be limited to six people, ideally three.

To end the discussion on corporations, let me also leave a very important note here for the people of any corporation, company, or organization. A study published in the Harvard Business Review discussed what it takes for companies to gain competitive and strategic advantage. It offered three dimensions of management: *quality (better)*, *time (faster)*, *and cost (cheaper)*—see Exhibit-G. Companies must put much greater emphasis on all three critical dimensions of success to survive or dominate the market.

They must significantly and constantly improve quality, reduce cost, and deliver faster in time. In order for them to dominate a market, they will have to score 10 out of 10 in all the three dimensions, because scoring 10 out of 10 in one or two out of the three will mean struggling to survive in this competitive business world.

The Challenges

We will have to face several difficult challenges, however. First, *human idiosyncrasies* or the people factor (see Exhibit-B) which are the most difficult. Next are *poverty and illiteracy* that are the root causes of all troubles and problems in the world today. In most cases, as Dr. W. Richard Bond—an

English-Canadian lecturer, Director of Distant Education at a Canadian university, and a dear good old friend—says, *illiteracy and poverty are caused by human greed, destruction of the middle classes, and political corruption.*

Next are, the bad religious gurus with destructive views <u>and</u> evil political leaders; these *people and power* abusers have made many people lose touch with the magic, beauty, and the real meaning of life and religion.

Another very pressing challenge is the *abuse of the name of religion*. Here are a few examples. The 9/11 episode of September 11, 2001, when "nineteen" hijackers using three out of the four hijacked American passenger jet airplanes as weapons attacked the United States of America (U.S.A.) by crashing the planes loaded with the rush hour passengers into its landmarks on the East coast.

The attacks on World Trade Center's twin towers in New York City and a portion of the Pentagon in Washington, D.C. killed thousands of people. A wing of the Pentagon's was destroyed and the WTC's two tallest buildings, with 110 floors each rising to over 1,350 feet (410 meters) with 10 million square feet of office space, were razed to the ground.

Other examples include the several decades old continuing struggles of: Jammu and Kashmir in the Himalayas of the East (Hindus vs. Muslims); Northern Ireland in the West (Catholics vs. Protestants); and the present very alarming situation in the Middle East (Jews vs. Christians and Muslims in Palestine, and elsewhere). Here are some details on these three struggles or challenges.

Jammu and Kashmir, generally known as Kashmir, is the most beautiful northern part (Himalayan Mountain range) of the Indian Subcontinent. The Subcontinent was partitioned into Pakistan and India in 1947 when it gained independence from Britain. The areas with clear Muslim majority were supposed to become part of Pakistan. This rule somehow did not apply to Kashmir, which has an overwhelming majority of Muslims, and consequently has resulted in a never-ending dispute between India and Pakistan.

Today, two-thirds of Kashmir is under Indian rule, and the rest is equally divided between Pakistan and China. Pakistan calls its portion Free Kashmir implying self-rule and has been working toward getting the same for the people of Kashmir living in the Indian portion. Both India (Hindus) and Pakistan (Muslims) have fought several major wars over it since 1947. Consequently, tens of thousands of people have been fatally victimized during, before, and after these wars.

The Northern Ireland conflict emerged as the result of years of escalating incidents between Catholics and

Protestants in the last century, with the involvement of a third party, the British. Thousands of people have been killed or injured in this conflict over the decades with seemingly no end in sight.

Finally, the most alarming situation in the Middle East, Palestine, where a Jewish state, Israel, was proclaimed in 1948 just before the British Mandate was to have expired. The Palestinian population, which is made up of a large majority of Christians and Muslims, were opposed to an Israeli State within Palestine. Later, as a reluctant compromise, the name of the issue was changed to "Partition of Palestine."

Today, the Palestinian people are simply struggling to create a Palestinian nation on whatever small portion of land is left of the original Palestine for Christians and Muslims. Gigantic human suffering on both sides (on per religious population basis) continue after many decades of struggle for a solution to the Palestinian problem, as does the influx of Jewish people from all over the world to Israel and to its many settlements. The Palestinian people very much appreciate the genuine sympathy that they have been getting lately from practically all the European and other countries around the world for their just cause. As for the present mediating U.S./U.K. leaders, Palestinians generally have little or no trust in them and some say that it's like having "poisonous snakes" as pets.

On the above three challenges (Kashmir, N. Ireland, and the Middle East), the people who always blame someone else for any wrongdoings are still debating if the British "divide and rule schemes" were a party to laying the trap of long term conflicts that potentially can lead to self-destruction. Closer to the fact on these conflicts, I am sure, are a number of factors, among them *people abusing the name of religion* on these three challenges that involve the people of four out of five major religions of the world.

As regards to the attacks on the U. S. on Tuesday, September 11, 2001, and since, it has stimulated public soul searching. Some American authors and lecturers are calling the unfortunate 9/11 episode a "useful crisis" with political connotations for the U.S. Administration. Unfortunately, the root cause of it all seemingly is being ignored, and the real mastermind behind these attacks on America has yet to be determined or publicly identified without a shadow of or reasonable doubt.

In reaction to the 9/11, September 11, 2001 attacks on America, in October 2001, U.S. with all its might went after to capture or kill one man of Saudi origin in Afghanistan. The man is Osama bin Laden, an extreme reactionary and strategist against what he believes the extreme injustice against and long suppression of his people in the

Middle East—U.S. called him an absolute suspect as the 9/11 mastermind.

However, U.S. has so far been unsuccessful to capture him, a millionaire who has chosen to live a primitive life by hiding in the caves of Afghanistan and has devoted the rest of his life to fight, as he calls it, the "infidels." In the process of trying to get this one man, however, U.S. killed or maimed thousands of innocent Afghan people who have had absolutely nothing to do with it.

Anyhow, the biggest question in people's minds right around the world even today is: Why did U.S. spare Saudi Arabia when fifteen out of the nineteen, as U.S. identified them, were from Saudi Arabia?

All this obviously raises more questions and speculations in religious and political circles, including the hundreds of thousands ordinary people in the U. S., as well as millions in Europe and billions around the world. Who actually executed the 9/11 operation appears to be somewhat clearer than the mystery of who was the real mastermind behind it. Was it an abuse of the name of religion? Was it instigated, behind the scene, by the wealthy and influential so-called lobbyists of ulterior motives? Well, the truth may not be known for decades, if ever.

Whoever is the real culprit for all the aforementioned challenges on earth and whatever the reason or motive, for example, *the oil and natural resource grabbing, the might is right, racism, supremacy, double standards, or religious and political conflicts*, these conundrums certainly have the wrong ingredients for a healthy society. If these enigmas go unchecked, they may eventually get the rest of the world powers involved in the most devastating armed conflict of all time.

Peaceful Means (The Just People)

Let's evolve the spirit and power of *just people* into a triumph of human beings who can overcome obstacles to fulfill our dreams of creating a peaceful world by using peaceful means. We must begin to work together to form more powerful coalitions and organizations around the world, organizations where people come together as equals and have the power to act together to achieve their right and just goals.

At the end of the day, therefore, it is the *just people power,* not the *nuclear power*, nor is it the *veto power* that will change the world for a better and peaceful place for all.

If we, the people who believe in the right and just cause do not wake-up to stop further bloodshed and sufferings in the name of religion, power, or politics, it may destroy the axis of our thousands of years old civilization and with it, humankind.

Using peaceful and nonviolent means, therefore, we must persistently and with determination lobby, march, do sit-ins, fast, or use some other more effective means to persuade all the powers directly or indirectly involved to tackle these conflicts by getting to the root causes of the *abuse of others* calamity instead.

The just people must demand a sincere, impartial, and concerted effort using peaceful means to make people learn to live as good neighbors. Make people respect each other's religious beliefs and understand the human right to exist with dignity in their own homes.

Finally, as an ambitious presidential craze, the U.S. is pushing ahead at an aggressive pace to have an air missile shield in place to shoot down enemy's long-range ballistic missiles. Three U.S. administrations, some critics call them the missile administrations, ironically, mainly from the same political party—the Republicans—have already spent heavily with a plan to spend a lot more in space-based missile defense technology. It spent billions of dollars just on researching the technology.

People must, therefore, try persuasively with determination to put an end to this enormously expensive U.S. air defense shield program that may never be utilized anyway. Tell them that it is no different to putting walls around the country as a defense against outside attacks or terrorism, which could still take place from within.

Besides, these protective shields or walls will never provide any guarantee against any attacks or any "ism," because the attackers can and will always find ways to beat the system. Therefore, we must make the current and future military-power-hungry or trigger-happy leaders to utilize that money for developing something more useful and worthwhile to protect their citizens, instead. So, *how about developing a **defense shield from those nasty hurricanes** that attack the U.S. every year?*

For a start, let's have a program that provides some financial assistance from the government for the homeowners to build very strong homes built perhaps of solid bricks in those southern U.S. states so that the people and properties are safe under those extreme conditions. The people of the United States will appreciate this a lot better than anything else the U.S. administrations have offered them in recent years.

As for the people around the world, let's make a sincere effort to move toward evolving a lasting peace that will virtually eliminate human suffering and current huge military expenditures. This means saving human lives and enormous savings in monetary terms. We can then utilize a fraction of these savings to fight other wars such as *reducing political and religious tensions* <u>and</u> *illiteracy and poverty* right around the globe.

Cardinal-Eight Simple Ways

One way to keep our heads above water is to come up with a list of key *simple ways* to handle difficult challenges facing humankind. Using the twenty-twenty vision, therefore, let's now look at the cardinal-eight *simple ways* for our survival, followed by some elaboration (what, how, and by whom) on each.

1. **Change, Change, Change**
    —Attitude, People, Systems, and Life
    —Tyrant Superpowers' Hellish Actions
2. **Stop the Abuse of Others**
    —Use the Strength of the Just
3. **Provide a Model *for* Right vs. Wrong**
4. **Facilitate Education to Eradicate Illiteracy**
5. **Check Extremism and Criticism**
6. **Create a World without Borders**
7. **Eliminate Scandals in High Places**
8. **Use Common Sense**

Now, let's elaborate each key **simple way** and hope that people around the world will make an attempt to accomplish at least some at first and eventually all.

1. Change, Change, Change
    —Attitude, People, Systems, and Life
    —Tyrant Superpowers' Hellish Actions

Don't be afraid of making decisions to change to reduce tension and stress, to gain competitive and strategic advantage in a business setting, or to simply survive and strive in the twenty-first century human and business jungle. No matter what our position (for or against) may be, change will make its course in the evolution of human striving.

Change may have taken place so slowly that it was not even felt in some generations, or it is occurring so rapidly today that we don't even notice it, or if we do then we are left somewhat overwhelmed by it all. However, there is no doubt of the important role that change is playing in contemporary society, and this high rate of change is nowhere more visible than in the technology field around the world. To survive and strive or simply remain competitive, individuals, groups, societies, corporations, and organizations cannot afford to stand still and, therefore, must go along with it.

Change in your own attitude is probably the key to changing other people (including the tyrants, religious gurus with destructive views, and others) and some of our systems like the legal, the health and welfare, and, in the process, to changing your own life.

So, begin by making decisions to come up with a more realistic strategic plan based on the guidelines offered in Exhibit-C: *Strategic Planning Process—The Society,* Exhibit-D: *Strategic Planning Model—Human Beings on Earth, and* Exhibit-E: **The Strategic Plan/Milestones—** Triumphant Society's Project of the Century. Test the plan and then follow it to evolve a peaceful world.

Without a proper plan is like shooting in the dark. Remember also that a plan is just a blueprint that will be needed but it won't deliver by itself. It will be the people— the teams of *just people* from around the globe—who will ensure that it can and will happen.

We need decisions now on political, religious, social, education, and other issues. Stop analyzing (ready-aim-aim-aim forever, never fire) and start experiencing (ready-aim-fire-aim-fire…) because when you fire and miss the target then you learn something from it to aim better the next time around.

There should be no doubt that due to the atrocities being committed by the tyrant superpower-lords' hellish actions around the world, there is an increasing number of people around the globe who are more than willing to change and influence those who might resist change.

Therefore, get an agent of change and an influential trustworthy leader or chief executive, I call that person the constructive "Godfather," to initiate the planning process so that our future generations can implement the much needed change for a better and peaceful world.

2. Stop the Abuse of Others
—Use the Strength of the Just

Utilizing the strength of the *just people*, we have to guide as some say the misguided few, who, with the influence of wealth and with some ulterior motives, constantly and skillfully lobby (bribe or brainwash) the most powerful *boys playing with their big toys.* Ensure that the boys are not being used as pawns. Make certain that wealth is not a factor when electing the boys for the big job, because in a true democracy, the right person for the job and human righteousness should be of greater importance than wealth and party politics.

Speaking of party politics, many people from the Eastern and the Southern regions of the world are very suspicious of some Western world's political parties and the hidden agenda of their founders who considered themselves as part of a superior race. Thus, they and their party's current prominent leaders and members are privately referred to as the "neo-Nazis."

Nevertheless, by using the *just people* strength or power, the biggest power of all, let's work toward ***stopping the*** *abuse of others* by the neo-Nazis, dictators, bad religious gurus with destructive views, tyrant superpower-lords, and evil leaders alike to end *their hellish action of creating a "man-made hell" on Earth.* Make them realize that justice by the Almighty, mightier than anything we will ever know, will prevail, as will love, brotherhood, and righteousness.

Today's superpower-lords (some American and European critics among others compare them with the Nazi Hitler and infidel Pharaohs), are also to be reminded of the tyrant supreme powers of the past eras. Here they are in chronological sequence: the Pharaohs of Egypt in 1400 BCE; the Holy Roman Empire during the first through the fifth centuries CE; Ummayad Rule—Yazeed of Arabia in the seventh century; the Genghis Khan dynasty (Chingis of NE China—Mongolia) of the thirteenth century.

Continuing with the tyrants of the past: the Mogul (Mughal) Empire of the Indian Subcontinent during the sixteenth through the nineteenth centuries; the British Empire from the sixteenth through the twentieth centuries (at its peak, the sun never set on the British Empire). Finally, Adolph Hitler of German Reich reined in Europe with his Nazism in the twentieth century CE. Hitler among other tyrants tried to exterminate Jews.

Ask the question, where are they now? The answer surely will have to be the Newtonian law of gravitation that got them all in the end; in layman's terms it is known as *what goes up, finally, must come down.*

These tyrants of the past in their long powerful eras and eventual downfalls, caused misery, destruction, bloodshed, and suppression with their lust of power and their desire to make people go tremendously astray. Therefore, no one has ever really cared to remember them except for the "para-historians" who write history in the way they wish it to be remembered. The greatest boxing legend, Mohammad Ali came up with an obvious summation of it, that is, history is precisely what its syllables show: "his and story."

As a final note, in the recent past decades superpowers managed to create a local little **monster** (e.g., Iraq's Saddam Hussein) or two in some regions of the world to serve their purpose. These little monsters in due course proved that they had their own agenda, because after years of subserviently committing atrocities in their own or neighboring countries (e.g., Saddam Hussein's war with Iran for a decade that killed or maimed tens of thousands of young men), they turned against their masters.

These masters or superpowers eventually have had to use their military might to easily destroy those little monsters (e.g., in Iraq and Afghanistan) they had created and, in the process, they killed thousands of innocent men, women, and children of the unfortunate lands without any feeling of guilt.

This inhumane attitude, as the perception has it, of treating the people from other lands like "ants or sheep" is at best a *win-lose* and certainly not a *win-win* situation. This attitude generates a million-fold more hatred right around the globe against the winner, if any; that simply means escalating the original problem and certainly not solving it.

The citizens of such so-called winner country—e.g., the U.S.A.—are so ashamed of all this these days that they try and hide their identity when travelling abroad, even when in Europe. As well, if you were to closely observe the faces of the occupiers' military personnel with all those guns and tanks, you'll notice that some of them look more scared than the local unarmed population.

The biased news media with little or no freedom of the press from the so-called winner country don't help the situation either when one of theirs in trouble gets the headlines but dozens, hundreds, or thousands of men, women, and children dead of the other side, barely make the news. This is not really surprising however, when the news media are controlled by a state. The state controlling the press (e.g., during the invasion of Iraq by the U.S. and Britain in 2003) was very disturbing for many in the Press circles around the world, including some very prominent and distinguished American people and journalists.

Among them, a legendary TV news anchorman, Walter Cronkite, whose famous last words at the end of the newscast each weekday night were *"That's the way it is."* In an interview on a TV network last year, Cronkite was also cynical about the term "em**bed**ded" ("in bed with 'em...") which was used by the U.S. Army for allowing the news reporters to travel with them in Iraq last year.

All that unfortunately has put a dent on the credibility of the U.S. news reporting media. The closest to unbiased and fair reporting in the English language today is offered by the world service news broadcast by the BBC, British Broadcasting Corporation, which is highly regarded worldwide for its reputation of telling it *the way it is*, a thing from the Walter Cronkite days, perhaps.

As far as the aforementioned never-ending world problems, I say that if we truly want to eliminate the above mentioned *win-lose* episodes then we simply have no choice but to get to the root causes of it all and find the way to make these unhealthy situations the *win-win* situations.

This viewpoint is shared by many around the Globe and the questions are raised among some political and religious circles, for example: Did these powerful nations not learn anything from it? How would they handle the militarily much bigger monsters they have created in the same or some other regions of the world, when they probably have to fight these big monsters one day to preserve their own military or nuclear supremacy? One of these big monsters or tiny little country, as an ambassador from a Western European country recently predicted, will trigger world war III involving the superpowers and all.

This war, if we don't try at all costs to avoid it, will kill or maim millions of civilians and hundreds of thousands of fighting young men and women soldiers. These military personnel, like in all the other wars, are dictated by a few so-called leaders sitting in their ivory towers, thousands of miles from the scenes of the battlegrounds.

I urge all the powers or super-powerful decision makers of the world to not let that happen to their own people and the rest of us, their fellow human beings, or to our future generations.

This will mean fewer military personnel who probably will have to stay in their barracks or at their bases to polish their boots everyday and keep fit to avoid boredom. Instead, to avoid boredom, I suggest that they do some worthwhile work by helping the communities cope with serious needs or problems of the ordinary people everyday and not wait until a disaster strikes. The super powerful nations, hopefully, will see some merits in all this what's been said here.

One such super-powerful nation in terms of military supremacy today is the United States of America—U.S.A. Generally, the people of the U.S.—known as Americans— are more and more isolating themselves from the rest of the world with their one-sided foreign policy and self-centered attitude. It is perhaps because of this attitude, that for many Americans, the rest of the world seemingly doesn't exist, including their neighboring countries in the North and the South.

Consequently, more and more countries around the world, including some European countries, appear to have stopped looking up to the U.S., as they may have done so in the past.

Are the Americans doing it all by design? For example, the name *"World Series"* in the top baseball leagues, where essentially all the teams are from the U.S. only, suggests that the answer to that question may be a yes. Surely, a base-ball team or two in these leagues are from outside the U.S., but these teams, for all intents and purposes, are owned by the Americans, anyway, basically for the purpose of making money. Besides the baseball teams, Americans also own many other businesses in their neighboring countries and in a number of other countries around the world.

The game of baseball, as a humorous note and before I talk about some positive things about the Americans, always reminds me of a much slower game called cricket. I enjoyed playing it a lot at a pretty good level myself when I lived in England and prior to that in Saudi Arabia. But suddenly I lost interest in it and I haven't touched a cricket bat in years.

While in Saudi Arabia, I was explaining the rules of this game to an American sitting beside me as we both were watching my team bat in a cricket match that was being played. Toward the end, I told him that it's a British game;...one cricket match at the international level lasts for five days and it usually ends as a draw, i.e. as a tie or with no result. His final comment besides "how boring and I can't take it anymore" was "now I know why the British lost their empire."

The recently introduced one-day international cricket match is certainly an improvement, but what I personally liked best was the half-day matches at the club level in England on weekends in a country club like setting. The families came out to watch it too and we all enjoyed it as a family picnic outing.

George Bernard Shaw (GBS), a dramatist and socialist from Ireland but spent many years last century in England always made fun of the game of cricket by saying that it's a game of fools. Here I would like to paraphrase his viewpoint to add my sense of humor a little. The bowler (pitcher) who runs a marathon race each time he bowls, throws, or pitches a ball <u>and</u> the batsman (batter) who waits from here to eternity to hit a ball after many deliveries (pitches) are the *big fools*. Once in a long while when the ball is finally hit then the fielders who chase it are the *bigger fools*, and the *biggest fools* are those who come to watch the game.

In England, during some several-day type matches, there are more pigeons watching the game than the cricket loving human fans.

GBS also used to make fun of the English language by spelling **Fish** as **Ghoti**. F or Gh as in rou<u>gh</u>, i or o as in w<u>o</u>men, and sh or ti as in <u>ti</u>on.

Now, back to the mighty Americans and their "business or investment wisdom." Having said all that about them before the cricket bit, I note that there are indeed some very positive attributes about Americans that should make the U.S. very proud of its people. For example, their work ethics, hard work, professionalism, and, in particular, their long term risky but wise investments in Research and Development (R&D) projects that have paid them back a million fold over a long period of time.

They are by no means perfect. But, having worked with the Americans for many years and physically lived and worked in the U.S. for several years, I for one can applaud them for their long term planning and foresight.

Once you have worked with them in the U.S.—tough, demanding, but fair and rewarding as they are, then you will have hard time in adjusting to another work environment. As for their professionalism, superior people skills, and exceptional customer service, they always have managed to hit the short list of three by the selection committees that I have been part of for multi-million dollar product search.

Furthermore, relative to most other countries—where there are much fewer jobs vs. the U.S., anyway—in which racism and prejudice are the norms against minorities in either very obvious or deceivingly subtle ways, U.S. generally puts more value on skills you have to offer than anything else. All this is part and parcel of their business wisdom.

Nevertheless, due to the unhealthy foundation that was laid by desolation of local original population and then forcefully bringing people from Africa for *slavery* in the eighteenth and nineteenth centuries, the United States like a few other countries in the world is still very much a racist society. This is despite the fact that significant improvements have been made in the last few decades mainly due to the fight for freedom, opportunity, and justice by the African-American Martin Luther King, Jr. King's famous "I

Have a Dream" speech is still widely talked about today, long after his assassination in 1968.

Regarding the American business wisdom, however, it is very unlike some other countries, for example, Canada, where businessmen believe in safe and short-term investment with guaranteed Return On Investment (ROI) almost "overnight." Examples of these businesses are banks and insurance companies that own practically all skyscrapers of any Canadian downtown.

Similarly, some other countries around the world with raw material economy, such as oil, are essentially ruled by one family or group whose wealth is many fold more benefiting to those countries where they do their banking. Unfortunately, this business or investment attitude potentially leads to a subservient setting.

It is of no surprise then that most of these countries particularly the neighboring countries of the U.S. so heavily depend on the U.S. investment and its economy. Simply put, when the United States economy gets a sneeze, meaning its economy is down a little, its branch plant subservient and economically dependent countries get pneumonia. Needless to say, the one suffering from a sneeze can recover fast, but the one with pneumonia may take a much longer time to recover, if at all.

Finally and relative to the Western European and some other more economically advanced countries with much higher cost and standard of living, North American (Canada, the U.S.A., and Mexico) economic situation is considered a turtle race today. Furthermore, an average Western European a few decades ago used to find a cheap vacation in the so-called "third world countries;" today, however, they all come to North America.

For the same reason, hardly anyone from Western Europe now wants to immigrate to North America, which is now attractive to immigrants or refugees from the third world countries only, and mostly those who are looking for jobs and for a few rich ones who are helping to create jobs.

These new immigrants prefer to stay in the greater metropolitan areas and thus have been lowering the standard of living considerably. Consequently, this influx is forcing many, particularly those of Western European origin to other fairly remote areas, closer to, as someone recently said, the American Indians who were pushed out there by the Europeans a couple of centuries ago.

Here with all the strengths and weaknesses or ills of our societies, I have tried to put across some very honest and constructive messages for all the people of the world with an eye on the *just people* to utilize their strength or power, the biggest power on Earth. Using the peaceful means, the just people of the world can help in persuading the tyrant super-power-lords and others alike from their hellish actions of creating a manmade hell on Earth. *We can do it*, that is, **stopping the abuse of others.**

3. Provide a Model *for* Right vs. Wrong

Using the best of my limited ability, here are a few words on the life of the magnificent seven religious, spiritual, and political Models of Life. We all should learn from the great examples of these superb life models, also known as Models for Right vs. Wrong. In chronological sequence, they are: Moses, The Buddha, Jesus Christ, Imam Hussain b. Ali, Mahatma Gandhi, Mao Tse Tung, and John F. Kennedy. Here are a few words on each; more details can be found in Chapter III.

Moses of the Land of Israel was one of the greatest figures of all the three religious books (the Torah, Bible, and Koran). Scripture states: "Moses was a very humble man; no prophet has risen in Israel like Moses; and that by faith, Moses chose to be mistreated along with the people of God rather than to enjoy the pleasure of sin with an evil ruler of Egypt—the Pharaoh and his treasures." In spite of his Egyptian upbringing, Moses always valued his Hebrew and Israelite background.

Moses will always be remembered as the one who drew out the people of Israel from the intense oppression of the Pharaoh of Egypt, about 1400 BCE.

Siddhartha Gautama (The Buddha, meaning the perfectly enlightened one) was born as a prince in a petty kingdom of the Himalayas (NE India) two and half thousand years ago. The suffering of living things were more and more engraved deeply into his life as he tried to understand the true meaning of human life. In his quest for peace and finding the root cause of the sufferings, he said, "Blood may become exhausted, flesh may decay, bones may fall apart, but I will not stop until I find the way to enlightenment."

At the age of thirty-five he at last found the path to enlightenment in India along the banks of the Ganges River, and the prince then became The Buddha—the perfectly enlightened one.

The reality of **Jesus Christ** of Nazareth is that he was completely a real human being, who was in every respect tempted by the devil "yet without sin." Jesus of Nazareth lived in Israel 2,000 years ago and died ("…died for three days…He will reappear on the Day *of* Judgment") when he was brutally crucified by the Jews and other accomplices like the Romans.

The first two commandments, from the words of Jesus Christ, are, "Love thy Lord your God with all your heart and with all your soul and with all your mind" **and** "Love your neighbor as yourself."

One of the greatest examples of someone who will be remembered until the end of time is **Imam Hussain b. Ali**, grandson of *Prophet Mohammed* of Mecca-Medina, Arabia. Imam Hussain provided a model for struggle between *right and wrong, good and evil, and truth and falsehood*. The Imam has a special status due to the great sacrifice of his family, friends, and life itself in the way of God, during a blockade of food and water for days in the sizzling hot desert of Karbala, Iraq. George Bernard Shaw wrote, "Islam is the best religion and Karbala's tragedy is its worst."

Mohandas K. **(Mahatma) Gandhi** of the Indian Subcontinent, "Man of the Millennium" was the twentieth century's unique visionary who *made things happen* by preaching nonviolence and by using peaceful means. The common factor of all religions, he voiced, is nonviolence. As the greatest spiritual influence, he had to earn the respect of his people first and eventually possessed the people power.

Mahatma Gandhi, it's refreshing to note, did not abuse his power. Instead, he assertively and convincingly persuaded most of his several hundred million people of the Indian Subcontinent in the East to use peaceful means and nonviolence to achieve their right and just goal of winning self rule from more than a century old British rule.

Before the British, it was the Mogul Empire that ruled the Subcontinent for three and a half centuries; both empires were very much royal family oriented and, therefore, did very little for the general public of the Indian Subcontinent.

Mao Tse Tung of China was born in a poor peasant family, later in 1920 became the principal of a school, and eventually after many years of struggle founded and rose to the position of Chairman of the Communist Party in China at the age of 56. Chairman Mao, as he was referred to by many, started a Cultural Revolution and had risen to rule a billion people. He unified China and oversaw the greatest social reform in human history. He was also a gentle and fair human being who once wrote, "Let a Hundred Flowers bloom, Let all the schools of thought contend."

He will be remembered as a socialist, a poet, and a military strategist. Mao Tse Tung certainly earned his place among the most powerful rulers of the world in the twentieth century CE

Lastly, **John F. Kennedy** (JFK) was the youngest elected president of the United States and was a charismatic, and magnificent leader in the mid twentieth century. He helped avoid a nuclear war and influenced the people of his time tremendously. JFK once said to his people, "Ask not what your country can do for you, ask what you can do for your country."

When JFK was assassinated (shot in the head by a "lone" gunman) in 1963 while as the 35th U.S. President he was traveling with a motorcade in an open car with his wife in a southern state of the U.S., the whole world wept. Today, after forty years, JFK is still remembered well right across the globe.

So, *to be remembered well,* not for any selfish reasons but as a good example of great human being, we should learn from these magnificent seven Models of Life to stop the *people and power* abuses, and all unjust religious or political wars.

The world can then save enormously in monetary terms on military, nuclear, and other arsenals. To repeat, we can utilize a fraction of these monetary savings to fight much bigger wars of *minimizing religious and political tensions* and *eradicating illiteracy and poverty* around the world.

4.   Facilitate Education to Eradicate Illiteracy

"Education for All," as UNESCO has it, is a human right. It's a key to freedom and development and, therefore, we need quality education that can enrich human life. To achieve overall quality in providing and facilitating proper education, we will have to make a concerted effort with an earnest desire of achieving excellence.

Jose Marti, a great poet and thinker, so very appropriately puts it, "All people, when they arrive on Earth, have a right to be educated; and then in return, they have the obligation to educate others." Marti continues, "To educate is to give people the keys to the world, which are independence and love; granting them the ability to walk alone, at the happy pace which is that of natural and free individuals."

Dr. Kalbe Sadiq, a scholar and visionary, emphasizes the need for education, science, and technology for the advancement and prosperity of all human beings. Proper planning for and the implementation of education, he says, can eradicate illiteracy, which is the root cause of all problems and troubles in the world today. The planning, as I understand it, is already there. What gets in the way of implementing it may be the real issue here.

Dr. Sadiq also points out that the majority of people from certain parts of the world are not doing enough about education that can eradicate illiteracy and poverty. Instead, they appear to be spending more time on judging others as to how well they recite the religious books. In most cases, reciting here does not necessarily mean that they understand the meaning or follow the messages within those useful books.

This is unfortunate because these magnificent books give very useful and practical guidelines on every aspect of life for all human beings.

Therefore, I urge the people of the world, particularly those from the world's Mid South East region who were once masters of the past many centuries but are now the so called "Have-nots" to try and understand the goal of knowledge. That is, as someone once said, the discovery of the truth and its utilization in the life of a human being.

Religion should not be a hindrance here but a close partner. They have to, like their current primary education system that is now second to none, begin using these guidelines for advancement through higher education, science, and technology to survive and strive in this competitive world.

As a part of the survival kit, they must also revisit other very important guidelines such as the one by the seventh century Commander of the faithful from Arabia, Imam Ali b. Abi Talib. Imam Ali said, "People deprived of knowledge will lose everything, and those who leave everything to acquire knowledge—through education—will gain everything."

As well, worth noting, is the great twentieth century German scientist Albert Einstein's belief that religion without science is lame, and science without religion is blind. Ignoring these guidelines, I am afraid, will mean that sooner or later their pride and dignity will cease to exist and they might even sink somewhere on this **Earth** without a trace. Well, the choice is theirs, or is it?

Speaking of **Earth**, here I would like to share an interesting point that certainly intrigues me. Why would God create human beings, "God's greatest creation," on this Earth, which is so very insignificant in the big picture of an infinite system of the universe? Another interesting point is that some people conclude that they are not interested in advancement through education and in the life on Earth; they would rather stay preoccupied with their own vision of **Heaven** and how to get there.

These people with their "conclusive" belief appear to be convinced that to get to **Heaven** is like competing in a marathon race on Earth; all religions are competing in it and one and only one religion will be the winner. People of each religion run the race, believing that they, being the chosen ones, will win the race and will at the end get to Heaven.

As Mirza A. B. K. Ghalib—a nineteenth century legendary poet of the Urdu and Persian languages from the Indian Subcontinent—put it, *"It's a good thought, Ghalib, to momentarily entertain the heart."* The first Prime Minister J. L. Nehru of Allahabad, India and his daughter Indira Gandhi, later a Prime Minister herself, among the millions others were very fond of this classic poet's work.

5. Check Extremism and Criticism

In most cases, **Extremism** stems at home during our childhood days. As we grow up, some of us fall into the category of a mild version of it all; others, unfortunately, develop these skills into a more serious category of extremism. Extremism, religious or political, over the centuries has resulted in serious conflicts leading to major wars. Millions of people, perhaps hundreds of millions, have been killed, slaughtered, or maimed because of that.

Nonetheless, the solution to the extremism lies somewhere in getting to the root causes of all first and then solving them. We cannot afford to let extremism flourish that in the end harms and even kills people. We certainly cannot continue to ignore the decades-old human suffering in the Middle East—Palestine, in the East—Kashmir, in the West—Northern Ireland, and the 9/11 episode of September 11, 2001 attacks on the U.S.A.

When we judge or use **negative criticism** of people or, for example, of another religion, it says nothing about that religion; it simply says something about our own need to be critical. It usually is a reaction, defensive act, or sheer jealousy—a confirmed ticket to hell.

Today, if we were to attend certain gatherings that are addressed by people of extreme views, we will, more often than not, listen to all the judgment and criticism that are typically levied against other religions or people. The impact of this on most people and certainly on people such as me is always nil or zero.

Being [negatively] critical does not solve anything; it actually misleads people and contributes to the anger and hatred in our world. A person who feels attacked, Dr. Richard Carlson says, is likely to do one of two things: he or she will either retreat in fear or shame, or more likely will attack or lash out in anger.

6. Create a World without Borders

We should work toward creating a world without any superficial or unnatural international borders that have come into existence mainly due to political, ideological, or religious conflicts. People would then be able to move freely anywhere (the North, South, East, and West) in the proposed *one country* world, as they do within a country, as we know it today.

Get a hint from globalization of the multinational corporations who set up branch plants in many different countries as if there were no international borders. These corporations, incidentally, don't salute any one particular national flag except for the green one.

Furthermore, we must have allegiance and loyalty to the part of the world (the North, South, East or West) we choose to live in without losing the values of our heritage. We have to get out of the religious or cultural inferiority-superiority complex mode and mix socially with others to learn and respect each other's background, culture, and religion.

The virtues I am discussing here may strike someone as utopia. Well, there may be another someone who would disagree to that. For many others, nevertheless, let's not stop our imagination from running wild in trying to achieve our goal of creating a world without any superficial or unnatural international borders.

One way to achieve *one country* world or a "global village" goal, perhaps, would be to somehow let today's militarily strongest country capture the whole world. When that has been done, use the strength of *just people power*, the biggest power of all, to change the attitude of the so-called rulers or occupiers.

Then, at some appropriate time, ask the occupiers to imagine themselves at their own funeral. It will allow them to look back at their life while they still have the chance to make some important changes. They will probably get a wake-up call that can make them do some good deeds toward fellow human beings.

Once the rulers start believing in service and good deeds to try to become great human beings, they will naturally provide for the rest of us some work, food, clothes, better standard of living, and education to eradicate poverty and illiteracy on Earth for creating a peaceful world.

Closest to our thoughts here is the Genghis Khan dynasty in the thirteenth century that covered a vast area from Mongolia, China through parts of Russia and Eastern Europe to Afghanistan, Iran, and the Middle East. The occupiers not only changed in many ways while in power but were also converted to the religions of the occupied lands. Another example is the British Empire that influenced the use of the English language as the *one language* for business world. Well, this may be a hint for creating *one country* world, a peaceful world without any superficial and unnatural international borders.

7. Eliminate Scandals in High Places

Religious high places or institutions around the world have some very dedicated people doing many good deeds toward fellow human beings. Some of these high places, however, are infected by a few deplorable scandals that will have to be eliminated for the religious institutions' future standing in the world.

Not long ago, these high places were known as, for example, God's church or God's mosque. Now, these are known as the Catholic Church or this or that church, and similarly, the Sunni or the Shi'a Mosque. Today, therefore, people are asking a very basic question, *Whatever happened to God?*

Well, the answer is not that easy. Bertrand Russell—a twentieth century British philosopher—said, "God did not create people but that people created God themselves to overcome their fears, such as fire, lightening, rain, earthquake,…food, life, and death." Bertrand Russell expresses his viewpoint here that is based on his belief of *the absence of evidence* about God's existence.

Religious people, however, might argue that the absence of evidence is not the evidence of absence. But then, long ago the religious people of the time had a hard time accepting the evidence about the Earth not being the center of the universe. Anyway, let's hope that soon there will be some evidence to satisfy both Russell's objections and the others.

As for the scandals in high places that people are talking about and that the news media have been exploiting recently, there are two specific scandals in these religious high places or institutions of the present time.

The first one is *"religious men sexually abusing minors and nuns"* and the other is *personal financial gain* using monetary contributions of the religiously faithful. Both of these scandals are to be addressed properly and promptly by getting to the root cause of it all, or the whole structure will sag of its own weight.

We need a logical and workable constitution (see Chapter VII for a proposal) in these high places to satisfy the law of nature and the biological and physiological needs. We also need a leader or mentor to change people's attitude and ethics in these places. People are to be constantly reminded of moral principles and the fear of God. The high places' future standing in the world depends on it.

8. Use Common Sense

Religious guidelines are mostly based on some common sense; let's use it. For the most part, believers should approach the Almighty as an individual on a daily basis. Well, we are born alone and we will die alone, then why not do this and a few other good things alone as well during our brief stay on Earth.

We certainly don't need a group or anyone else, however more knowledgeable, as an interpreter when trying to approach the Almighty. We should have the utmost respect for those with greater knowledge and know-how about religious, political, or other activities; however, we are not to be intimidated by them in any way, shape, or form. These knowledgeable and learned people have no more or less direct approach to God than any other individual.

Individual or group setting here in this context may be an issue for those who obviously need help. Each individual should use common sense and must learn to think (see

Exhibit-J Religious Truth.) without the influence of the blind faith. Time and time again we hear people say that they finally found a book, a glorious book that puts it all together for them. So for those needing help, try and read it among other books yourself and then decide. If you cannot read, then ask someone else to read it to you in a language you understand.

As regards to the individual or group dilemma, well, for Dr. W. Richard Bond, a scholar and lecturer with good knowledge of several religions, *individual or group* is a non-issue. He points out, however, that the group settings have certain purposes and advantages such as creating social structures, networks, and marriages. It's interesting to note, however, that neither the individual, nor the group is exclusively important. What's important is a combination of both.

Finally, people often say to me "…but it is true" because they heard someone say it or they actually read it somewhere. My first question to them usually is "who told it or who wrote it?" Because, while we should certainly listen to people and read what someone has written on a subject that interests us, we should always keep in mind that we don't necessarily have to believe in everything we hear or read.

This is due to the fact that most people tell stories based on their biases, likes, and dislikes. For example, try listening to the radio and TV stations or reading the newspapers of two different countries at war with each other; you would most probably get two different accounts or even opposite stories about the same incident.

The only way to get the true story is to further investigate (if it's really necessary) or use your own judgment and, yes, use common sense. Ideally, though, we should have a mind that is open to everything and attached to nothing.

Conclusion

The discussion of power, politics, religions, people, and life ends with some consideration of what appears to be current trends in the social, political, cultural, and religious thoughts. Some questions are raised concerning the values about people's proper role in a society increasingly characterized by large and powerful political or religious groups.

On the very shaky assumption that agreement can be reached on this role, there remains the very complex, practical question of how to go about achieving the desired results. To achieve the end results, nevertheless, the ideas or the cardinal-eight *simple ways* that have been developed here can be used as more than just guidelines or framework within which a more detailed *"how to"* plan and an implementation strategy can be constituted by those wishing to make life meaningful.

The attitudes portrayed and arguments developed here are simply an intent on my part to present viewpoints in a fairly brief way somewhere short of gross exaggeration so as to show the differences and the significance of differences in the mother of all realities—different cultures, religions, and people. The assumption here is that people tend to lean toward one extreme or another, the side they favor being determined by their current situations, their particular socialization, and their general political, cultural, and religious ideologies.

This is not intended to suggest that most people fall into extreme categories; rather, the argument is that most people lean one way or another, and this is quite important for both the proposal here in this book and the implementation later by the just people around the globe. Furthermore, people can easily or unconsciously be quite inconsistent in their views.

Nevertheless, believe in your own religion's vision and values that teach us the meaning of life and ask us to always wish well for fellow human beings. This, in essence, conveys that as great human beings for *making life meaningful,* we accept and respect different people, religions, and cultures.

I encourage the people of the world to consider deeply *The Life Model* (see Exhibit-A) and realize that we are all very different, they should truly understand and honor the fact that it literally can't be any other way. I urge more and more people to crave for truth and spread it around the world, as well, make a plea to the Almighty to make us great human beings for making life meaningful.

Again, once we have truly earned the supreme level as great human beings, the love we feel for people, the respect we have for other religions and cultures, and the level of compassion we have for our own religion's uniqueness will increase dramatically to the ultimate goal of treasuring life.

As for the realistic level of expectations, peace on Earth is not something we will achieve overnight or even in our life-time. It will be a long-term struggle with eventual victory, perhaps over a few generations when there will be all new people.

Religions, as I understand it, are supposed to eliminate per-sonal conflicts and control our impulses. They also put *greater emphasis on doing good deeds toward fellow human beings than on worshipping God.* That, in the final analysis, as well as learning from the aforementioned magnificent seven grand religious, spiritual, and political Models of Life are the keys to begin a glorious journey toward developing a passion for people to make life meaningful, and to gain inner and lasting peace.

Will there be a Day of Judgment? "If there is going to be the Day of Judgment," Anwer A. Zaidi, a friend of mine, points out, "the utmost question that God will ask us will be about our dealings with all the people we have interacted with in our lifetime. If we fail in that, we will fail miserably. On the other hand, if there will be no such Day then it simply doesn't matter."

Can the religions get along? Well, the one man who holds the key to our possible reconciliation is the Model of Sacrifice—*Abraham*—(known as Avraham in Judaism and Ibrahim in Islam). Abraham defines faith for half the population on all six continents of the world. Abraham's offering a son to God plays a pivotal role in Christianity at Easter, in Judaism on Rosh Hashanah, and in Islam as the Feast of the Sacrifice at the climax of the Pilgrimage. "*Abraham*," as Bruce Feiler wrote, "relates to contemporary religious and political conflicts…there is still a hope that may redefine what we think about our neighbors, our future, and ourselves."

The strategies to evolve a peaceful world will have to be developed by the **just people** of the world, based on the persuasive guidelines provided here in the form of *"simple ways to handle difficult challenges"* that have been explored throughout in this book.

The challenges such as attitude, change, people, extremism, illiteracy, and poverty, as well as tyrants' hellish actions, destructive religious gurus, scandals in high places, and the abuse of others will have to be handled with determination and conviction to succeed in the creation of a peaceful world. World without any superficial or unnatural international borders.

As for the blueprints of strategic planning process—the society, strategic planning model—human beings, and strategic plan/milestones—triumphant society's project of the century, see Exhibits C, D, and E, respectively.

Finally, while we are thinking about strategies, the implementation of these strategies can wait. What we cannot wait for any longer, however, is to begin the process of strategic planning, forming the implementation teams, and education.

Simply initiate this process now so that someday the people of our future generations can make our book's title *So Close, Yet So Far Apart—Stopping the Abuse of Others*, a thing of the past.

Treasure Life

___:___:___:___

II.

Change, Change, Change

—Attitude, People, Systems, and Life
—Tyrant Superpowers' Hellish Actions

One of the most important conditions necessary for the successful initiation and the implementation of change is when people are under stress with more than normal tension, like they are today due to *the abuse of others* right around the world. As well, the individuals or groups that are willing to change due to stress or tension must put all their forces to assertively overcome those who resist change.

Furthermore, at the world level, like in an organization or corporation, someone must gain the acceptance and support of all including those who resist change or feel threatened by it.

In my own experience of successfully introducing change—information technology (IT) and change I believe are mutually inclusive, the initiation always came from someone who was universally respected and trusted. The people who needed confidence that the change can make the difference to survive or even strive in today's competitive business jungle, were persuaded by the influence, position, and judgement of a senior executive or chief executive, who I called the "Godfather" in a constructive sense.

So, change your *attitude* to change other *people* (including the bad religious gurus and tyrants and their hellish actions, as discussed in Chapter I) and, in the process, change your own *life*. In today's world, worth noting, change is so rapid that we are overwhelmed by it, or some of us don't even notice it.

Nevertheless, accept change to get energized and not paralyzed. A concerted effort to change from the narrow mindedness to an *open mind* blessing will be required, not so much to win rewards but as a way of life.

Remember that there is a difference between an *open mind* and a hole in the head. As well, bear in mind the message from the Serenity Prayer: Change the things that can be changed, accept those that cannot, and have the wisdom to know the difference.

Stop putting up any roadblocks or blaming your circumstances. George Bernard Shaw so appropriately wrote, "People are always blaming their circumstances, I don't believe in circumstances. The people who get on in this world are the people who get up and look for circumstances they want, and, if they can't find them, make them." Make a real effort to be someone who either makes things happen or watches things happen to learn from them. But we should not be like someone else who asks, what happened?

Continuing with the theme of change, I would also like to share a few words on discrimination, for example, against women in our society today. It's a man's world, despite significant achievements by women to correct that discrimination and inequality in the last several decades.

The English language, authors of the past, and business owners and corporations are as much to blame for following this idiosyncrasy, when you see words like: s<u>he</u> from he, <u>man</u>kind, hu<u>man</u>, per<u>son</u>, chair<u>man</u>, wo<u>man</u>, and even God is referred to as He. This is just a very simple example to prove who were and still are controlling all this, that is, men.

If you are still not convinced, then as my observation has it, make a business trip on an airplane in, for example, North America today. You'll find that the business travelers, mostly executives, are overwhelmingly and predominantly men.

Men of the past and present with power have seemingly made you feel as if the reality of the feminine or soft gender doesn't mean anything. Ask these men, where would they be without a woman, a mother, or wife?

Men and women are different in many ways; and we should thank God for that. Furthermore, each and every individual in your life including your own children has a different place from your own perspective. These differences of individual personality, ability, intelligence, and character should and will be here to stay. This type of difference is not the issue. The issue here is the discrimination and racism that are based on people's gender, religion, or outer layer of their skin.

Based on some perception in the West, women are even more suppressed in the East. Similarly, as the perception has it in the East, men and women in the West have little or no sexual morality. Well, having lived in the West for decades with my roots in the East, I can say with some certainty that there is very little truth in both cases. People from the West, on morality issue, follow the same moral principles as they exist anywhere else in the world.

Besides, who are "we" to make judgements, set morals, and come up with standards while sitting thousands of miles apart?

This reminds me of a documentary I watched years ago about an American missionary in some remote place in

South America. The missionary was there to try to civilize some American Indians who lived there very happily in the most serene and perfectly natural environment. I have never observed a more content and happy people anywhere. But before the American missionary left, the people of that remote area began to worry about clothes, stove, electricity, TV and radio, and everything else that certainly were not part of their good old contended life.

As regards to the other perception, women in the East or South East not only rule at the home front but a great majority of them, behind the scene, participate equally on every issue of the eastern society. On some issues, nothing moves without their approval. As the recent historical facts have it, eastern countries have had more women leaders of prominent political parties or Prime Ministers than in any other part of the world.

Due to some prejudices and narrow mindedness, mix marriages (East and West) are not welcomed in some snobbish circles in the West, nor are these appreciated in the East, where there are further restrictions even for those prospective couples who are part of the same religious sect. Arranged marriages are still quite common in the East, and amazingly enough tying the knot to be partners for life, "till death us do part," is so strong that it seems to last longer than through any other system.

That's the good news, the bad news is that parents of the bride and groom in the East (in some countries, time has no value, e.g., eight o'clock sharp means eleven o'clock start) spend their lifetime savings on far too many marriage ceremonies and feasts. There are two big such ceremonial feasts that are usually attended by hundreds and even thousands of people, but these are usually more like wasting food occasions than enjoy eating it. Because some of the guests are always complaining about the quality of food and many leave half of the food in their plates that they had topped up to start with.

Anyway, at the end of it all, some parents in the East go totally broke and join the ranks of the poor, who are also under pressure to keep up with this unhealthy show off tradition that makes their young folks wait for ever to get married.

Speaking of marriages, some countries in the East allow more than one spouse (currently it is "wife") if the population proportion of male and female truly dictates it, and if they can treat the second or more spouses equally, among other very strict rules. Very few, therefore, qualify and not more than 0.00001% of the population can actually afford it. So, you have to go a long way to find anyone having more than one spouse.

Someone from the West once jokingly or sarcastically said to a chap from the East that he really likes the system of having more than one wife. The chap from the East, also jokingly or in retaliation to that remark said, and I quote: "but I prefer the Western system of one wife or husband with a few mistresses or lovers."

This conversation and some of the wrong perceptions, unfortunately, are part of the *"us and them"* feeling that has been created both by past and present troublemakers with destructive views. Pity!

For a world (East or West, North or South) with equality, fairness, and no discrimination, people who believe in the right and just cause will have to do a lot more than they have done to date. They have to handle the troublemakers and discriminators (men or women) who obviously are suffering from some inferiority-superiority complex.

Above all, we have to pity them, deplore them, and not to be intimidated by them, because if we were to take their clothes off, or remove the outer layer of their skin, we will find that they are no different from anyone else.

No one should have the supreme treatment in deed or in our minds, not even the royal families. If we want to put a family up there for ceremonial purposes then people can understand that, but making them super human beings or making them financially rich are what people are questioning these days. Furthermore, look at the history of some of these royal families and see for yourself how they got there. You will find that some of them did not have a very moral or healthy background to the point that they are referred to as power hungry monsters, outlaws, or robbers by some historians.

We must also check and deplore any *"cast and untouchable"* systems, which are not much different to the equally deplorable *class categorization* such as upper, middle, and lower, as well, for example, House of Lords vs. House of Commons.

To share my own experiences in Saudi Arabia, Americans of this large oil company were classified as "upper class" and were provided first class accommodations with superb facilities for living, sports, and entertainment areas. People of other nationalities (with very few exceptions, e.g., a few doctors) working for the same outfit were classified as "intermediates" or "others" and were provided more than adequate but relatively second class facilities. Americans were also not allowed to socialize with the intermediates and others. Isn't that a class system? Isn't this like today's other class or racist systems deplorable?

As for fairness, we must have a closer look at one specific area that is being associated with workplaces, such as the hospitals (nurses and doctors), banks (tellers and managers), and factories (production line workers and supervisors).

While we should continue to value the doctors, managers, and supervisors, we must at the very least, equally appreciate and value the nurses, the tellers, and the line workers for their hard work and the service they provide day in and day out without any perks or executive lunch hours.

Other areas needing change are today's health and welfare systems that are being badly abused, as well as change in our legal system where people are getting away with murder if they can afford to hire a really good lawyer. Lawyers also write the laws of the land in a language only they can understand. Now, that to me is like asking inmates to write the rules of our prison systems.

Regarding the gross abuses of the welfare and other similar systems, those who had introduced the systems many generations ago certainly had the genuinely poor and the needy people in mind. However, with today's abuses of it, it probably makes those good old folks turn over in their graves every day.

These systems were designed to accumulate money for the needy from the contributions of the working people who sweat blood over decades for their livelihood and, in the process, have helped the welfare and other systems. The common sense, therefore, tells us that no one should be entitled to any financial or other similar assistance until they have had contributions made to the systems long enough or have lived in the country for a minimum of let's say twenty years.

In some depressed areas, people have been drawing money from the welfare system for generations. Some new arrivals or families immigrating to a welfare state start banging the welfare office doors or telephoning the welfare office immediately after they land at the state's international airport for financial help.

Whether they get some financial support day one or later, whether they get it temporarily or for generations, these are not the issues. The issue here is, whether those who even genuinely qualify for it—through their length of contributions or stay in the country—be entertained at all unless the healthy ones are made to work or do something worthwhile for the community they live in.

Furthermore, the system allows you to get financial help if your cash or bank account gets to a certain low level with no job; other factors such as owning a million-dollar home or owning a Mercedes Benz or two are simply ignored. Well, you might be saying and I can almost hear you, why? We obviously have to stop this welfare abuse or else we will have little left in the kitty for those who are and will be entitled to it, in a real sense. Let's at the very least think of those who have been making contributions all their life; simply help to stop the abuse.

Lastly, the strengths and weaknesses of our health system or medical profession in the so-called developed countries in particular and around the globe in general. While we should respect the medical doctors for their higher education and what they do for us, we should not be putting them way up there in the professional ladder.

One doctor friend, who, incidentally, is one of the top heart surgeons in town, once said to me, "A doctor is simply like a car mechanic or computer technician and he or she, because of his or her long years of education and training, is pretty good at it. However, the doctors generally have no concept of managing people or place. Think twice, before putting them, with some exceptions of course, in a management or administrative position, unless you want to make a real mess of a hospital, politically and administratively speaking."

As for the weaknesses in the health system, I would like to share a very personal story. My ten-year young daughter (Anne) is a pleasant lady of few words; she hardly ever speaks a word or two and even that is an echo from someone. She is suffering from some serious health problem or brain defect. All MRI and other tests show normal results. We have gone through many assessments, endless assessments by the specialists who seem to do that very well, but diagnosis and treatment have so far been royally nil and majestically zero.

After our persuasive arguments, medical specialists have somehow agreed that Anne is not truly autistic and have, therefore, defaulted to significant *developmental delay* (DD) as the diagnosis. Anyhow, I personally believe that Anne's diagnosis should be no-development (ND) rather than DD. DD meaning developmental delay to someone like me implies that one can retain something on a delayed basis. Anne, unfortunately, has not retained much of anything in ten years.

Anyway, once Anne's mom and dad are gone, she would probably live with some community agencies that have so far been fairly adequately supportive to our beloved daughter's situation and her needs. What she really needs now is a brain surgery but that may be a thing of the twenty-second century.

Anne, as a final note, has been on the waiting lists for this or that for years to get help, for example, from a speech pathologist or an autism specialist but by the time she gets to the top of the list, she is declared as too old. Ironically though, these very specialists, if contacted privately, are available literally the next day or the next week. The confusing setting of medical specialists working for a hospital and practicing privately on their own elsewhere would probably be declared as "conflict of interest" in a corporate setting.

Having said all these not so good things about the health system and its practitioners, we simply cannot live without them. Despite the fact that today's family physician's role is limited to prescribing antibiotic and, for anything slightly serious, referring you to a specialist who is usually not available for months (by then perhaps you won't need them anyway), the health systems have come a long way in the last century.

Thanks to the overall development in the medical field, more lives are being saved today and people now live healthier and longer than ever before. Today's medicine, however, like the militarily powerful political leaders, are effective only at the surface level for a temporary relief and do not, in most cases, remove the root of it all for a permanent cure.

This is especially true for the seriously ill people or very old folks, who somehow end up in old people's homes for the remaining few years of their life when they truly would like to be close to their family as never before.

I would, therefore, like to make a personal appeal to today's societies to help eliminate most of the old people's homes, and to try to make the old folks live where they really belong, their children's homes. Due to moral obligations and in a willing effort to keep the family unit living together as a unit, having the old folks at their family home is still a common practice in many healthy societies around the world.

Despite some inconveniences or impracticalities, and barring some very seriously ill old folks, it can be done if their sons and daughters try to sacrifice <u>a little</u> for their old parents who over the years sacrificed <u>a lot</u> for them.

For example, my sister and niece—my real heroes—had my parents in their homes until my old folks passed away peacefully when they were around the ninety year mark. My father was always fairly healthy but my mother, worth noting, suffered a stroke and was in pretty bad shape in her last years.

To truly appreciate all what I am trying to convey here, visit an old people's home, talk to some of these old folks, and look into their eyes to experience it all first-hand, as I have. Here then, I would like to share a very touching story.

In one old people's home, a good old English lady once told me that life is not a straight line, and that it always has some ups and downs. Over the years, we, pointing to her husband in a wheel chair, have had our share of these ups and downs like many other couples. But the difference between some others and us is that when we were done fighting over some little silly things, we never sulked over it for more than a couple of days that seemingly were unending hellish days in our lives.

We certainly did not go to the extreme of breaking up our marriage, she continued. We stayed together partly because of our family unit of four to keep it together as a family unit. "But you know what Syed," she said in concluding with tears in her eyes, our family unit is no more as we have ended up here in this crummy old people's home and our two sons with their families are elsewhere. They do visit us once every two to three months, if we are lucky.

I say, it's a very sad reality in some unhealthy societies that I have just shared with my readers. We must, therefore, change all that like the other ills in our society such as tyrant superpowers' hellish actions of creating a manmade hell on Earth.

Using the just people strength, we must stop the "boys" from playing with their big toys and, in addition, ensure that they are not being used as pawns by those possessing wealth and having some ulterior motives. Let's stop the misery, bloodshed, destruction, and suppression so that people can enjoy the beauty and the real meaning of life on Earth.

As I have said it before and I'll say it again, *we can do it.* Working together, the just people should come up with a realistic long-term "*how to*" strategic plan and the implementation strategy, based on the strong guidelines and framework or blueprint (see Exhibits-C, D, and E for the planning process, model, and the milestones for the triumphant society, respectively).

To help achieve our goals, Chapter—I specifically outlines the cardinal-eight *simple ways* to change the world to make it a better place to live for all. We should use agents of change and the constructive Godfathers. People will have to accept the winds of change; the choice for them is not whether, but how to do it.

Treasure Life

___:___:___:___

III.

Great Human Beings

Models *for* Right vs. Wrong

Any model for right vs. wrong or of a great human being must satisfy two distinct demands. First, the model must be sufficiently simple to allow us to organize facts about life and human beings, and to make sense of what we observe. Second, the model must be complete enough to be an accurate predictor of effort and performance (the outcome of people interacting with people) in actual individual, cultural, or group settings.

In addition, I would also like to encourage people to use common sense and faith (not blind faith) with an open mind in making decisions about individuals, groups, religious, or cultural behavior.

The models I have chosen to purposely present again with more detail in this chapter compared with Chapter—I are the magnificent seven religious, spiritual, and political Models of Life and Models for Right vs. Wrong. All human beings from every corner of the world must be able to make sense of what they observe and organize the facts about life from the examples of these great and complete models.

Here they are, in reverse chronological order: John F. Kennedy of the United States, Mahatma Gandhi of the Indian Subcontinent, Mao Tse Tung of China, Imam Hussain b. Ali of Arabia, Jesus Christ of Nazareth, The Buddha of the Himalayas, and Moses of the Land of Israel.

John F. Kennedy (JFK), was part of a large and rich family from Hyanis Port, Massachusetts. He was the youngest elected president of the U.S. as well as a charismatic and magnificent leader in the mid-twentieth century. He helped avoid a nuclear war and influenced the people of his time tremendously. JFK once said to his people, "Ask not what your country can do for you, ask what you can do for your country."

When JFK was assassinated (shot in the head by a "lone" gunman; people still talk about it as a conspiracy) in 1963 while as the 35th President, he was traveling with a motorcade in an open car with his wife in Dallas, Texas, the whole world wept. A veteran TV anchorman, Walter Cronkite, wept on a national U.S. television network during the news broadcast, as well. Considering that these newscasters are well trained not to show any emotions while on the air, this also touched many hearts in North America and elsewhere.

The funeral procession and the burial ceremony in Washington, D.C. also were the most touching such episodes in the U.S. history. In particular, a "sad looking" horse (JFK was very fond of the horse that was given to him by the people of Pakistan) walking with the procession without its beloved rider, and above all, JFK's two year old son, JFK Jr. bidding farewell to his father with a brave salute. The Jr. grew up to be a very pleasant and charming person; unfortunately though, he died in a plane crash recently while piloting the plane himself.

JFK's younger brother, Senator Robert F. Kennedy after winning the California Primary was shot and killed in 1968; theories have it that he was also a victim of some conspiracy. Another brother, Senator Edward M. Kennedy who is one of the most prominent senators today may have toyed with the idea of running for the presidency of the United States but has so far been staying away from it all.

My father was so saddened by JFK's assassination that he wrote a very touching letter of condolence to JFK's wife (now Late) Jackie Kennedy, who personally acknowledged it with deep and sincere thanks. Both documents can be found in John F. Kennedy Library, Boston, Massachusetts.

My late father always admired JFK and had great respect for the U.S. and its achievements. He often very fondly talked about his American teachers at an American school in Allahabad, India. He once told us that one of his teachers wanted to take him to the United States because of his "unique and most beautiful singing voice" but my grandparents didn't want to have any of it. Some of us may have inherited my dad's voice. Interested anyone?

Anyway, for my family like millions of people around the world, John F. Kennedy will always be close to our hearts and certainly will be well remembered as a great human being.

Mohandas K. **(Mahatma) Gandhi,** Man of the Millennium, was the greatest spiritual influence. He believed in his vision and certainly was someone who *made things happen* by preaching nonviolence and by using peaceful means to achieve independence or self-rule from Britain. The common factor of all religions, he voiced, is nonviolence. To keep his people of different faith and religions together as one, he often said, "I am a Christian, a Muslim, a Hindu, and a Sikh."

For Gandhi, it may have been and probably was easy to practice more than one religion, as well as to preach the same to his people of the Indian Subcontinent in the East. With due greatest respect however, for the rest of us folks in this world, it does not seem to be a very practical proposition, nor is it a realistic one.

Closer to reality is the acceptance of the principle of *different realities,* which conveys that the people-made differences among religions are every bit as extensive as the differences among many cultures around the globe. "It is not a matter of merely tolerating the differences," to quote Dr. Richard Carlson, "but of truly understanding and honoring the fact that it literally can't be any other way."

Despite Gandhi's remarkable and extraordinary efforts to keep the Subcontinent in the East together as one country, it was partitioned into two countries—India and Pakistan—in 1947 due to the people-made major differences between two predominant religions (Hinduism and Islam). Ironically, differences among religions (e.g., between Judaism and Christianity or Islam) were again the major factors for creating a new country Israel in 1948 in the Middle East. In the West, Northern Ireland may also be heading for a similar destiny for its two Christian sects (Catholicism and Protestantism).

Mahatma Gandhi, nevertheless, accepted the reality of different religions and cultures and respected them all. He certainly was one of the great human beings of the twentieth century.

Gandhi was shot and killed by a Hindu extremist in 1948. Interestingly enough, his other half for getting the independence from Britain, M. A. Jinnah—the founder of Pakistan—also passed away the same year. While Gandhi fought for independence by walking with his people on the streets, Jinnah, England's Oxford University trained successful lawyer, used a different approach by convincingly debating it all in the rulers' boardrooms for not only independence like Gandhi but a separate country in support of his fellow Muslim compatriots.

The final result of all this was independence from Britain with a partition of the Indian Subcontinent in 1947 into India and Pakistan. Pakistan relatively speaking consisted of areas with the least educated people. As for the independence, it was allowed partly due to the fact that Labor Party of Britain was the elected government at the time and not the Conservative party which many people believe would have never even considered giving up the British "Raj" or rule.

However, the consequence of this independence during the initial stages was that millions of people were forced to leave their homes with literally nothing, to migrate in both directions. Hundreds of thousands of men, women, and children were slaughtered, killed, or maimed in the process by the rival religious fanatics, extremists, or uneducated people.

Gandhi and Jinnah both succeeded in their quest for independence from the foreign rule however. While Gandhi's India today is seemingly enjoying it as the world's largest democratic system, Pakistan has so far been, thanks to the several ambitious army generals and their successful coups, struggling or somehow surviving in that arena.

Pakistan also lost its eastern wing in 1971 giving birth to a new nation, Bangladesh, mainly due to the fact that one particular group from its Western wing was dominating both wings (the West and the East). This group may not be the very highly educated people in the world but it controls the arms and the army. They are certainly good soldiers, hard working people, and very resourceful indeed.

Nevertheless, the rest of the people in today's Pakistan—that partly consists of those who seemingly do very little but complain a lot—are still wondering as to which one is worse, the former British rule or the current new rulers from within. Many people in Pakistan today also sadly mention the abuse of Jinnah's guidelines on unity, faith, and discipline.

As for the democracy, I personally believe that copying a democratic system from one part of the world is not necessarily the right thing for some other regions of our globe. What we need in some of these regions and for that matter anywhere in the world is an honest, strong, and charismatic leader that I call a "constructive dictator," like the word constructive is used with criticism which is one of the most appreciative gesture anyone can get.

When I see people voting for a crooked or unworthy person just because he or she belongs to the political party they like, then it convinces me even more to say that the party politics is not what a country needs.

Furthermore, people who need more education on the subject are often asking questions about those elected to the parliaments or senates. Questions such as, what do these parliamentarians or senators do? In most cases, are they simply keeping the seats warm? Are they woken up once in a while to say "yea" or "nay" based on what is being dictated by the party or do they act based on what makes sense and is good for the country? People obviously need some answers.

Anyway, Mahatma Gandhi, whose India may have many problems and challenges for its nationals of a billion people, but it appears to be doing reasonably well with its present democratic system. He was certainly a *model for right vs. wrong*. Gandhi for all his humanly divine approach and good deeds will be remembered well for a very long period of time.

Mao Tse Tung was born in a poor peasant family. In 1920, he became the principal of a school, and eventually after many years of struggle founded and became the Chairman of the Communist Party in China at the age of 56. He overthrew an army of four million strong and ruled China for over twenty-five years.

Chairman Mao, as he was referred to by many, started a Cultural Revolution and had risen to rule a billion people. He unified China and oversaw the greatest social reform in human history, and may have been the most powerful person who has ever lived. Mao was also a peaceful and fair man, as he once said, "Let a hundred flowers bloom, and let all the schools of thought contend." The transformation of China was so rapid that in 1953 a group of foreigners were pleasantly shocked at the rate by which the country had transformed. Mao, however, was not so pleased.

Mao Tse Tung laid the foundation for China to be the next superpower; he certainly earned his place among the most powerful rulers of the world in the twentieth century CE. He will be remembered as a socialist, a poet, and a military strategist.

The greatest example of someone who will be remembered well until the end of time is ***Imam Hussain b. Ali***, grandson of *Prophet Mohammed from Mecca-Medina, Arabia*. Imam Hussain *provided a model for struggle between right and wrong, v*irtue and vice, good and evil, and truth and falsehood. The Imam has a special status due to the great sacrifice of his family (including a "six month old" baby son), friends, wealth, and his life itself in the way of God. Yes, he sacrificed it all during the water and food blockade for days in the sizzling hot desert of Karbala, Iraq.

George Bernard Shaw, a great philosopher, wrote, "Islam is the best religion and Karbala's tragedy is its worst."

Imam Hussain and his small group of men were forced to fight and were martyred against amoral forces in the thousands, as the Imam refused to legitimize an evil Ummayad ruler Yazeed—worse than the Pharaoh's—in the seventh century CE. A reporter in his commentary describing God's compassion said, "The heavens did not weep for the death of anyone except for an ancient martyr John of Zachariah and Imam Hussain b. Ali. Its redness [at sunset] is the sign of its weeping."

Jesus Christ is the central figure of Christianity. He was born in Bethlehem in Judea, and Christian church regards him as "Son of God" and the redeemer of all humanity. The religious authorities (Judaism and Paganism) about 2,000 years ago saw him as a threat, hated him, conspired with the local Roman civil authorities, and eventually put Him to death or—as the holy books say—crucified him.

The reality of Jesus Christ, as it is recorded in credible and holy books, is that he was completely a real human being, who was in every respect tempted by the devil "yet without sin." Jesus of Nazareth lived and died when he was brutally crucified ("died for three days…He will reappear on the Day of Judgment") in Israel 2,000 years ago. He will be accompanied, as Shi'a Muslims believe, by Islam's twelfth and last Imam, Imam Mehdi. Jesus Christ's first two commandments were, "Love thy Lord your God with all your heart and with all your soul, and with all your mind," and "Love your neighbor as yourself."

To continue with Jesus Christ's words, "I did not come to abolish the Law or the Prophets, but to fulfill them," and "If you have faith as small as mustard seed, you can say to this mountain, move from here to there, and it will move. Nothing will be impossible for you."

As a final example, we take; his well known encounter with a Samaritan woman at Jacob's Well in Samaria's city of Sychar while He was on a journey from Judea (Jerusalem) to Galilee (Nazareth). He asked the woman for a drink of water and later said to her, "I who speaks to you is He [Messiah or Christ]…God is spirit, and those who worship Him must worship in spirit and truth."

Siddhartha Gautama (The Buddha, meaning the per-fectly enlightened one) was born as a prince in a petty king-dom of the Himalayas (NE India) two and a half thousand years ago. The sufferings of living things were more and more cut deeply into his life as he tried to understand the true meaning of human life. In his quest for peace and to find the root cause for the sufferings, he said, "Blood may become exhausted, flesh may decay, bones may fall apart, but I will not stop until I find the way to enlightenment."

At the age of thirty-five he at last found the path of enlightenment in India along the banks of the Ganges River, and the prince then became The Buddha—the perfectly enlightened one.

It was an intense struggle for forty-five years for The Buddha to pass on his findings and beliefs, among them, for example, four Noble Truths and Eightfold Path to people. Today, however, 150 to 200 million Buddhists are spread out around the world but mostly in the East.

The Four Noble Truths as a central theme of The Buddha are: 1. Life is frustrating and painful. 2. Suffering has a cause (we are constantly struggling to survive). 3. The cause of suffering can be ended, by being a just, simple, direct, and straightforward person. 4. Meditation is the way to end cause of suffering. The Eightfold Path: Right view, right intention, right speech, right discipline, right livelihood, right effort, right concentration, and right absorption.

Lastly, **Moses** lived around 1400 BCE. His father had named him Chavier and his grandfather called him Avigdor, but the name Moses, meaning "take out," was given to him by Pharaoh's daughter. He always showed deep, almost obsessive commitment to fighting injustice.

Moses is one of the greatest figures in all three glorious religious books (the Torah, Bible, and Koran). According to these books, He received the Ten Commandments of Judaism from God on Mount Sinai.

Scripture states, "Moses was a very humble man, no prophet has risen in Israel like Moses, and that by faith, Moses chose to be mistreated along with the people of God rather than to enjoy the pleasure of sin with an evil ruler of Egypt—the Pharaoh—and his treasures."

In spite of his Egyptian upbringing, Moses always valued his Hebrew and Israelite background. Moses will always be remembered as the leader of the Exodus from Egypt and thereby the founder of Israel. He certainly is one who drew out the people of Israel from the intense oppression of the Pharaoh of Egypt several thousand years ago.

Now, as you may have observed, most of these seven Models for Right vs. Wrong were either assassinated or crucified. This goes to show that the evil conspirators simply wouldn't let the good human beings move in the right direction, the direction of peace and tranquility.

Today, however, it's refreshing to hear visionaries state the belief that we are not Catholic and not Protestant but we are Christian. Similarly, it's good to listen to scholars and visionaries, like Dr. Kalbe Sadiq, who say that we are not Sunni and not Shi'a but we are Muslim.

Unfortunately though, these visionaries have stopped short of explicitly mentioning the *supreme level*, great human being, as depicted in *The Life Model*. If we were able to reach that supreme level in the true sense, then by staying within our own religious beliefs or boundaries, we should be able to *accept the mother of all realities*—different people, religions, and cultures—by respecting all other people, religions, groups, and cultures on Earth.

All major religions of the world share this viewpoint and have profound similarities in their key message or golden rule. For example, one such rule states: Not one of you truly believes until you wish for others what you wish for yourself.

Other major religions convey the same key message, their golden rule, with slightly different wordings. All this should make us **so close, yet** because people so *mercilessly* have been abusing other people, it has made us **so far apart**. That, in essence, is the real issue at hand here.

In my humble attempt to convey a clear message, let me take us all to that *supreme level*. Imagine, just for a moment, that you are not a Buddhist, Christian, Hindu, Jew, or Muslim but first you would like to become a great human being to make *life* meaningful. If we were to achieve a fraction of that goal in the true sense, then, by staying within our own religious beliefs and boundaries, we would begin to *accept and respect the reality of different people, religions, and cultures* on this Earth. This would also raise the level of compassion we have for our own religion as good Buddhist, good Christian, good Hindu, good Jew, or good Muslim.

Surely it will take time and sincere striving on peoples' part to even reach the starting point of achieving that goal, a very tall order. To succeed in accomplishing the critical strategies for a peaceful world, more than just a good effort will be required, as the good cannot be accepted as good enough in the twenty-first century. Only excellence will be acceptable as good enough.

For critical self-examination and to succeed in achieving our objectives here, we have to also start taking everything we do personally. We need to make a personal commitment to excellence in everything we try to accomplish. We will face many challenges and hurdles, such as the human idiosyncrasies or the people factor (see Exhibit-B), being the most difficult. Some will put up roadblocks and others will simply blame their circumstances.

This is because practically all of us are so totally conditioned by identified social structures from the day we are born that it is almost impossible to even minutely change our way of life and our blind faith without an extraordinarily purposeful and goal directed plan. Nevertheless, always remember that the people who get on in this world are the people who get up and look for the circumstances they want, and, if they can't find them, make them.

Anyway, let's begin. First of all, we must eradicate illiteracy and poverty, the root causes of all the troubles and problems today, by promoting and facilitating education, science, and technology. Second, accept change and then change people and systems; check extremism, criticism, and scandals; and help create a world without any superficial or unnatural international borders.

Third, use the strength of *just people power* for **stopping the abuse of others**. Remove the *people and power* abusers, the *bad* religious gurus with extreme and destructive views, and the tyrant political and trigger happy leaders who in some cases perhaps are being used as pawns by those with wealth, wrong influence, and with ulterior motives. They have made so many people completely lose touch with the magic and beauty of religion and life.

Lastly, we must accept the principle of *different realities* to respect other people, religions, and cultures as the key for becoming great human beings to make life meaningful. This will lead us to enjoy inner and lasting peace that we all need for our survival in today's world.

Regarding to the principle of *different realities*, I have seen an understanding of some of it change people's lives. During their childhood days in an ideal setting, no one particular religion was forced upon them. They were not discouraged either about getting to know or practicing the good things of any religions of their own choice.

In another setting, children can be brought up to follow their parents' faith or religion with an emphasis on the great human being aspect of it all in the true sense. This combination, I am sure, will lead them to accept and respect the *mother of all realities*—different people, religions, and cultures. It will make them reasonably happy people and it can virtually eliminate any prejudice, quarrel, negative criticism, or extremism.

Finally, do provide service and good deeds, and don't tell anyone about it or expect anything back in return because, when we do, we always notice a beautiful feeling of ease and inner peace. For example: do a good deed without expecting a seat in Heaven in return; do praise God without expecting God to fulfill your needs in return;…do go to other people's funeral without expecting other people to come to yours in return.

I may be one of those who talk or write about these things more than providing some action, but I personally know a few people who actually practice exactly what I am talking about here. Among others for example, my younger brother, a first cousin, and their families living in the Toronto area do provide good deeds without expecting anything back in return. Remember that love is not love that asks for a return.

Simply do it *anyway,* as the word *anyway* is used in a lovely poem below by Mother Teresa, one of the world's greatest humanitarians known throughout the world for her charity toward the poor and her firm and passionate pro life stance to make *life* meaningful. Thanks to a friend, Anwer A. Zaidi, for providing me this poem by Mother Teresa. Here it is then, enjoy reading it as I do, anyway.

- *People are often unreasonable, illogical, and self centered; forgive them anyway.*

- *If you are kind, people may accuse you of being selfish with ulterior motives; be kind anyway.*

- *If you are successful, you will win some false friends and some true enemies; succeed anyway.*

- *If you are honest and frank, people may cheat you; be honest and frank anyway.*

- *What you spent years building, someone could destroy overnight; build anyway.*

- *If you find serenity and happiness, they may be jealous; be happy anyway.*

- *The good you do today, people will often forget tomorrow; do the good anyway.*

- *Give the world your best and it may never be enough; give the world your best anyway.*

- *You see, in the final analysis, it is between you and God; it was never between you and them anyway.*

Treasure Life

___:___:___:___

IV.

Education *for* Eradicating Illiteracy

As I was about to finish writing this chapter, UNESCO began holding an International Education Conference in Geneva, Switzerland with over a hundred Education Ministers attending the conference from countries around the world. It was also honoring an International Literacy Day 2004. I was simply delighted to listen to Director-General of UNESCO International Literacy, Koichiro Matsuura, emphasize the need for quality education. He was calling upon all countries, rich and poor, partner agencies in the United Nations, bilateral and private donors, and, indeed, private citizens everywhere, to make sure that the word *"illiteracy"* is eradicated from our vocabulary.

Education for All, as UNESCO has it, is a human right. It's a key to freedom and development. Quality of education, as some of us know it, can enrich human life. To achieve quality, however, we must have an earnest desire to achieve excellence; nowhere it is needed more than in the field of education.

Furthermore, as Matsuura emphasized, quality is not just about academic knowledge and achievements, important though they may be. It is clear that the modern world is demanding much more of education; it is counting on education systems to build the foundations of a better world, one based on universal values of peace and equality. I say, bravo!

It is refreshing also to quote Jose Marti, a great Cuban poet and thinker, who so very appropriately puts it: "All people, when they arrive on Earth, have a right to be educated; and then in return, they have the obligation to educate others." He continues, "To educate is to give people the keys to the world, which are independence and love; granting them the ability to walk alone, at the happy pace which is that of natural and free individuals."

Dr. Kalbe Sadiq, a scholar and visionary from India, emphasizes the need for education, science, and technology for the advancement and prosperity of all human beings. Proper planning for and the implementation of education, he says, can eradicate illiteracy and poverty which are the root causes of all the troubles and problems in the world today. The planning, as I understand it, is already in place. What gets in the way of implementing it may be the real issue here.

Dr. Sadiq also points out that certain parts of the world, particularly the East and South East, are not doing enough to provide and facilitate proper education. Instead, they appear to be spending more time in judging others as to how well they recite some religious books. In most cases, unfortunately, reciting here does not necessarily mean that they understand the meaning of great messages within those glorious books.

In this vital area of education, there will have to be a wake-up call for the people of the world. This specifically applies to the people of the East and South East regions, who were once masters of the past many centuries but are now the so called Have-nots, or they will sink somewhere on this Earth without a trace. Well, the choice is theirs or is it?

The East or Southeast regions, as part of the Southern half of the world, particularly their narrow-minded religious gurus and many others with closed mind and blind faith might argue that it is least interested in advancement and life on Earth. These so few gurus and their misled so many, instead, may prefer to stay preoccupied with the notion of their own vision of Heaven and how to get there.

Incidentally, Earth as we know, is a small part of our solar system; which is a very small part of our Milky Way galaxy, which has over 250 billion stars or solar systems alone. As far as the scientists know, there are billions and billions of galaxies in the universe. This makes our Earth to be the most insignificant entity in the infinitely big picture of the whole universe. So, why did God choose Earth for human beings, which, as the self-praising has it, people believe is God's greatest creation?

As for getting to Heaven, interestingly enough, it is like a marathon race where all religions appear to be competing with a belief that one and only the winner will be allowed to get there. The followers of each religion strongly believe that they, being the chosen ones, will win the race. Well, as Mirza Ghalib, one of the great poets, puts it, *"It's a good thought, Ghalib, to momentarily entertain the heart."*

People often say to me that if those who are only interested in Heaven and don't want to be part of any advancement on Earth through education, science, and technology, then let's ask them not to travel by airplane, train, automobile, bicycle or even donkey carts. They should go back to the plain old donkey and camel days for traveling from A to B. Furthermore, they should not use telephone, electricity, electronics, radio and TV, computers, modern medicine, and surgical apparatus.

Realistically speaking though, people have no choice but to change and once again begin using their own religions' guidelines that emphasize the need for advancement through education. I would, therefore, like to urge all those in the Southern region of the world that have fallen behind in this arena to act fast and to begin the long and most essential journey now in order for them to survive and strive in this world.

Once again, as an essential ingredient for our survival and advancement, it is imperative that we understand the goal of knowledge, as described by someone as *the discovery of the truth and its utilization in the life of a human being*. We must also understand that, as Imam Ali said, people deprived of knowledge will lose everything, and those who leave everything to acquire knowledge—through education—will gain everything.

The people of the South have no choice but to move forward and prepare for the big change. It will not be an easy task to change their own attitude and that of others from their own and other parts of the world. In the process, however, they will change their own life for the better. Nevertheless, use change as an opportunity to get energized and not paralyzed. As for providing quality education, a concerted effort of the magnitude of achieving excellence by all will be needed, not so much to win rewards but as a way of life.

Finally, seriously consider the message from Albert Einstein, a great German scientist, who recognized the need for education, science, and religion to be close partners by stating that *religion without science is lame, and science without religion is blind.*

Treasure Life

___:___:___:___

V.

Extremism and Criticism

Extremism comes in many ways, shapes, or forms. It comes in also as political, religious, and personal criticism. We may be living in a so-called free society, but mentally we may not be free. So, extremists can devastate us mentally as well. As one of the credible books has it, extremism exposes us to danger and insecurity. As for my opinion, I always believed that extremism stems from hate breading hate.

Examples of extremism during world war II were: Japan's bombing of Pearl Harbor's U.S. Naval establishments; Americans putting Japanese Americans into concentration camps; and then the U.S. going to the extreme of dropping atomic bombs on August 6 and 9, 1945 on Hiroshima and Nagasaki, Japan. This act of dropping atomic bombs on civilians was considered by billions of people around the world as a barbaric act. Americans, however, defended it by arguing that this was the only way to stop the Japanese, who, incidentally, were about to surrender, anyway.

The race for developing nuclear or atomic bomb, as an extremely destructive weapon, was on between Hitler's Germany and the U.S.A. The U.S. obviously won the race that helped them to win the war by going to the extreme of dropping atomic bombs on Japan. This victory was not only for the U.S. itself but for its European allies as well. Surely anything that threatens our people must be checked and checked well, but going to the extreme is what is the real issue here.

Communism was also felt by some as a threat for over fifty years in the twentieth century and people were arrested just because their neighbors either disliked them or felt and reported that they were communists. Today, terrorism is felt as another threat. Are we also going to be scared of it for another fifty years? Would we put up walls around our countries to protect our people?

Well, I hope not. Because that will not be a guarantee against terrorism or any other "ism." Today's terrorism that kills a number of people each day of the week, the one we hear about constantly as if the world has no other newsworthy items, is highly deplorable to the nth degree and more. It's also repeatedly happening between people of the same religion but of different religious sects. Shame!

However, if we were to put the weight on numbers killed, it is a much smaller number when compared with the number of people killed, mugged, terrorized, murdered, and abused each day in, for example, some major cities in North America alone.

As well, every other word used by some of the leaders these days is terrorism or terrorists. It is not because of their limited vocabulary but because they feel it's necessary to tell the world something about them and, you know what, the terrorists probably love it every time the word *"terrorists"* is mentioned by these powerful leaders and by their news media.

Furthermore, these leaders and their news media immediately blame the whole nation, religion, or the race for any extreme act by an individual or a small group who may happen to have been born in or associated with one of those places that are somehow on their blacklist. On the other hand, if it is someone like, for example, Timothy McVeigh who bombed a day care center in Oklahoma City, U.S.A. in 1995, killing many children and some adults, then the buck somehow always stops at the McVeigh's.

Today's deplorable terrorism has come into existence because of decades of many frustrations but mainly due to the fact that powerful nations have been taking side with one people and ignoring the other. It is, however, only a drop in the bucket when you consider the powerful nations that have been terrorizing the whole *weaker nations* around the world for years and centuries. Furthermore, the *weaker nations* are often used by the superpowers to satisfy their political needs of the time and then are simply dumped when the needs have been fulfilled. All that and more gives birth to many-fold more terrorism and extremism around the world.

I am often saddened when I see people, as part of their extremism, discriminating people of other religions, religious sects, or beliefs. They don't allow marriages between people of the same religion but of different sects. Worse still, they don't eat each other's food and often go to the extreme to avoid even touching someone they believe is untouchable. Depending upon whom they touched or brushed by, they wash their hands once, twice, three times, or even have a royal bath to purify their body again.

Without a doubt in my mind, all this is contrary to the guidelines of any religion that came into existence for the good of the people. It's the people, however, who under this very sacred umbrella have gone to the extreme of making religion what it is not supposed to be. Millions, perhaps hundreds of millions of people have been killed, slaughtered, or maimed over the past centuries because of some religious and political extremism or conflict.

Today, it is still happening in the East (Kashmir), the Middle East (Palestine), and the West (Northern Ireland);

each one incidentally is perceived by some, who always find someone else to blame, as a *British* creation for their *"divide and rule"* schemes. Well, here we go again, **criticism**.

Yes, we all at times *negatively criticize*, too. But when people point out this weakness most people have, we should really feel bad. The solution is to catch yourself in the act of being negatively critical. Quite often then we can turn our criticism into tolerance and respect.

So, in searching for the grain of truth about the *British* mentioned earlier regarding *"their divide and rule"* schemes, first ask ourselves these questions. Could these schemes have been created by some other sources? Why did the people of these lands allow themselves to fall into this, as some call it a trap?

The trap, ironically, by whoever is so strong that religious quarrels and troubles continue today even after decades of British or whomever else's disappearance from these lands.

When we expect to see things differently, when we take it as a given that others will do and react differently to the same stimuli, the compassion we have for ourselves, for our own religious beliefs, and for others rises dramatically to treasure life. The moment we expect otherwise, as Dr. Richard Carlson says, the potential for conflict or criticism exists.

Criticism here implies ***destructive criticism,*** and certainly <u>not</u> the constructive criticism that we should always welcome.

When we judge or criticize another religion, it says nothing about that religion; it merely says something about our own need to be critical. Dr. W. Richard Bond, a scholar, lecturer, and instrumental in the important area of distant education says that most religions typically don't criticize other religions, barring a few misled bad groups or speakers.

Dr. Bond, a family friend and an inspiration to us all regarding education and willpower, has first hand experience with and good knowledge of several religions, including those very bad groups or individuals who have destructive or extreme views. He now lives near Hamilton, Ontario, Canada but we have known each other since the 1960s, the years of our good old days in London, England, where my older brother spent several years in the late 1950s getting his training from the British Royal Air Force.

Based on my own experiences, if we were to attend certain gatherings that are addressed by speakers of extreme or negative views, we will, more often than not, listen to all the judgment and criticism that are typically levied against other religions or beliefs. After the gathering, when we go home and consider how much good all that criticism actually does, we always come up with the same answer: nil, zero!

Being critical does not solve anything; it actually misleads people and contributes to the anger, hatred, and distrust in our world. A person who feels attacked, as Dr. Richard Carlson says, is likely to do one of two things: he or she will either retreat in fear, shame, or more likely will attack or lash out in anger.

Treasure Life

___:___:___:___

VI.

A World without Borders

The world would be a better place for all of us if there were none of the current superficial or unnatural international borders that in most cases have been created because of the political, ideological, or religious conflicts. It would also be healthier for all human beings if they were allowed to move freely anywhere they wanted to go and live in the world (the North, South, East, or West), as they freely do within a country as we know it today.

If we were to study the history of the countries of the world, we will find that most of these countries or nations with their current international borders are the result of some political or religious conflicts—see Exhibit-I Global Political Systems. The current disturbing situation in the Middle East, as we all know, has everything to do with political and religious quarrels and differences.

This conflict may eventually involve countries from the rest of the world in destroying their own world. The only way to prevent this disaster of catastrophic magnitude is to ask the just people of the world to wake-up and use the strength of the *just people power*, the biggest power of all, for *stopping the abuse of others*.

All the people of the world will have to directly get involved in a peace move that not only convinces the parties directly involved in the conflict in the Middle East but also those who are known as the "boys playing with their big toys."

Let's guide the trigger-happy *boys* as some describe the misguided few who are perhaps the victims of those with wealth and some ulterior motives; these rich and wealthy instigators with their agents constantly use the superpower-lords as pawns and always skillfully lobby, bribe, or brain-wash them.

Make certain that wealth is not a factor when electing these boys for the big job, because in a true democracy, electing the right person and human righteousness should be of greater importance than party politics.

Then, by using the strength of *just people* power, persuade the dictators, tyrant political leaders, bad religious gurus of destructive views, and the madmen alike to stop the hellish action of creating a manmade hell on Earth. Let's make them realize that justice by the almighty, mightier than anything else we will ever know, will prevail, as will the love, kindness, righteousness, and brotherhood.

Today's superpower-lords are also to be reminded of the tyrant powers of the past eras, such as the Pharaoh's, the Holy Roman Empire, Ummayad Rule—Yazeed, Genghis Khan dynasty, the Mogul Empire, the British Empire, and the Nazism of Adolph Hitler's German Reich.

Ask the question, where are they now? The answer surely in almost all cases will have to be the Newtonian Law of gravitation that got them all in the end; in layman's term it is known as *what goes up, finally, must come down*. In these long eras and final downfalls, power and people were abused. Destruction, misery, bloodshed and suppression had been caused by tyrants' lust of power and their desire to make people go tremendously astray.

Therefore, no one has ever really cared to remember them except for the "para historians" who write history in the way they wish it to be remembered. The greatest boxing legend Mohammad Ali came up with an obvious summation of it, history is precisely what its syllables show: his and story.

Among all the supreme powers of the past, the British relatively speaking were a little more humane. They appear to be somewhat hanging in there today due to their English language, which is now accepted as the one language for the business world. Well, this may be a hint toward creating *one country world*.

Anyway, working toward the goal of creating a world without any superficial or unnatural international borders, the just people should also guide others, the rest of the population on Earth, to *accept the mother of all realities* and *respect different people, religions, and cultures*, to gain *inner and lasting peace.*

Failing that, I am afraid, the axis of our civilization of the past thousands of years may be destroyed and with it, humankind. That's the bad news; the good news, however, is that the strength of the just people power can stop this *hellish scenario of a possible manmade hell on Earth.*

In a world without borders, there would be no need for any embassies, international border posts, passports or visas, customs and immigration nonsense, wars, military, and gun or nuclear arsenal expenditure. Hence, we can have enormous savings for the one country world. These savings, I am sure, would be more than enough to educate and to raise the standard of living for the entire population on Earth, "God's chosen place for humankind."

Today's superpowers are so strong that they can and do harass and capture almost any country at will. For justification, hypocrisy, double standard, lobbying (some call it bribing or brainwashing) and the might is always right play definite roles when we hear that, except for the chosen few, other countries can't have destructive arsenal because they might use it.

Well, if destructive arsenals including atomic bombs are not to be used, then why should we have it at all anywhere, including the one and only one country, the U.S.A., that has actually used it to date by dropping it on Japan, during World War II last century?

So, the powerful countries can win any war against most countries. They can do so only with a fraction of their military force, nuclear, and other arsenal. They may even call that a great achievement or success and then celebrate. In the final analysis, however, the win against the little guys would be classified as bullish and certainly not an achievement.

The much bigger war to win and then to deservedly celebrate would be the *elimination of religious or political tension* **and** *eradication of illiteracy and poverty* within the superpowers' own countries and indeed throughout the world.

Undoubtedly then, if today's superpowers were to spend a fraction of their military arsenal money and effort on the betterment of human beings of their own countries and the entire world, poverty and illiteracy around the globe would be wiped out within a reasonable period of time. This will naturally lead to harmony and peace on Earth.

Perhaps, the rest of the world should let today's one superpower have the oil and whatever other natural resources they want, and let it rule the entire world. Then, at some appropriate time, ask these rulers to imagine themselves at their own funeral. It will allow them to look back at their life while they still have the chance to make some important changes.

They will probably get a wake-up call that can make them do some good deeds toward fellow human beings. Hopefully, they might one day become more human and decide to help fellow human beings by trying to eliminate poverty and illiteracy, hence; raising the world's standard of living. It might sooner or later also lead us toward creating a world without borders.

Continuing with our theme here, let's have a word or two about the **North** (the "Haves" of today) and the **South** (who were once masters of the past many centuries, but are now the so-called "Have-nots") regions of the globe. This is a division that is used by large corporations for their globalization interest.

Our globe's North has dramatically advanced mainly due to the proper use of education, science, and technology during the last century or two. Religion here does not appear to be a hindrance but perhaps a close partner.

The South with a very high level of illiteracy and poverty particularly in the mid South East region, on the other hand, as Dr. Kalbe Sadiq tells us appears to be spending more time on judging people as to how well they recite the religious books.

Reciting here in most cases does not necessarily mean that they understand the meaning or the message within those glorious holy books. This is unfortunate because these grand books give the most useful and superb guidelines on every aspect of life for all human beings.

The North, thanks to its advanced technology and know-how, is also getting richer at the expense of the poor by selling its products to South. Products such as banking services (the biggest money making and, at times, freezing business), airplanes, jet fighters, guns, tanks, automobiles, electronics, radio and TV, computers, information and the internet or e-mail technology, and higher education, which it provides even in the North, as well.

The good news about higher education is that some people, a very small fraction of the grand population from the South, are able to achieve it in the good colleges and universities of the North. The bad news, however, is that once these people become highly educated and trained, or that when the time comes for the South to reap the benefits, they decide to stay in the North; most succeed.

Those who succeed in staying up North or those who immigrate to or find refuge there in a multicultural and multi-religious setting are provided a safer and a better place to work and live with their families.

Some of the countries in the North, worth noting, do accommodate or provide all this mainly because they need the manpower from abroad. But, it is partly because the human spirit still exists there; they are also usually the first to provide not just the financial help but their people support to help people elsewhere when a natural or any other major disaster occurs.

Continuing with the North, some of these countries here also provide free medical coverage for all those living within the country. Practically all these countries grant free basic education and have good facilities for higher education for those who have the brain for it and can afford to spend money, effort, and years in a higher educational institution.

The immigrants, refugees, and others with the freedom of practicing their own religion, their standard of living is raised a notch or two. After several years of residency in the North they even get the nationalities of the countries they chose to live in. Most if not all of this obviously was unavailable in these people's own countries of origin, or in some other in transit country in the Southeast or Middle East (e.g., Saudi Arabia), where in many cases, ironically, the religion practiced is predominantly the same as theirs.

Speaking of religion, suddenly in September 2004, it was announced that there is no freedom of religion in Saudi Arabia. This is not a new discovery because it has been known for decades. What's new and probably alarming for the country mentioned, however, is that the current U.S. administration at the highest level has chosen to speak out about it now.

Saudis, as Syria and Iran that are repeatedly accused of developing "nuclear and other programs," must be wondering if this is the beginning of a similar plot or scheme that led to the invasion of Iraq by the U.S. and Britain in 2003.

One big question in many minds these days is: Are some other countries of the same religion surrounding this region on the hit list as well? These powers ("military, not necessarily the wisdom") always say, with a straight face and perhaps believing that the world is so naive, that they are doing it all not because of religious conflicts, one sided diplomacy, oil revenue, or the control of other natural resources but to stabilize the region.

People of the world, however, are saying that these powerful nations can fool this region or the world sometimes but not all the time. The same people also believe that the leaders of these powerful nations are being constantly bribed or brainwashed by those neo-Nazis or "*Nazis in reverse*" with wealth and some ulterior motives. These terms are not to be confused with Hitler's Nazism.

The term *Nazis in reverse* I have used here because if you were to look at the history of the world, you will find that those who were suppressed by other nations, groups, or individuals, are pretty good at suppressing others when the situation reverses over time.

A very good example in support of this statement is the past hundreds of years of history of the tiny islands called the British Isles. Before Britain became an empire during the sixteenth to the twentieth century, it itself was conquered and ruled by several other powers for centuries. Britain—at its peak, the sun never set on the British Empire—obviously did a pretty good job of using the same tactics or strategies they learnt from their masters of the past.

Anyway, if today's powerful nations were really sincere about the stability in the region of the Middle East, then they should begin disarming the country or countries of the region and indeed of the world that have already had the nuclear arsenal at their disposal for years.

Now back to the people who find refuge in the West or up North, many of these people don't appear to have as much allegiance to or loyalty for their host countries as they should.

Due to some inferiority-superiority complex about their own religion, culture, or whatever, they also don't mix with the local demographic population much. They prefer to live close to and spend practically all of their free time with people of their own religion, culture, and background from predominantly their old country—a very narrow-minded attitude.

Even within these narrow-minded settings, the power, politics, jealousy (the biggest curse), and personality conflicts are majestically flourishing. People from the same religious sect but of different background and language are often trying to "cut each other's throat," or close to it. If you are a recent convert then the chances are that you will be praised on the surface but will be looked down upon as second class citizen in people's minds and certainly will not be socially accepted as one of them.

Maintaining their culture and religion or holding on to the values of their heritage is perfectly fine. However, people must get themselves out of narrow-minded inferiority or superiority complex mode and make an honest attempt to mix socially with and truly respect others of different background, culture, and religion.

Above all, they ought to have the loyalty for their host country that has provided them a safer and better place to live, work, and, among other things, raise their families with religious freedom. All the aforementioned essential ingredients are the first steps toward eventually creating *A World without Borders*.

Treasure Life

____:____:____:____

VII.

Scandals in High Places

Before getting into specific scandals involving many religious high places or institutions right around the globe, let me say that these places have some very dedicated people doing a lot of good deeds toward fellow human beings. Their whole life is devoted to nothing but serving people.

As for the high places, however, let's try and remember that these places originally were known, for example, as God's church or God's mosque. The church has now become the Catholic Church, this church or that church. Similarly, the mosque has become a Sunni Mosque, Shi'a Mosque, or some other mosque. Some of us are, therefore, asking one very basic question: *Whatever happened to God?*

Well, the answer to this question is not that simple. Bertrand Russell believed, due to the *absence of any real evidence,* that God did not create people but that people created God themselves to overcome their fears, such as fire, lightening, rain, earthquake, food, life, and death. Needless to say, despite the universal high respect for Bertrand Russell as a great British philosopher, this viewpoint does not fly very well with any religious group. Religious people argue that the absence of evidence is not the evidence of absence.

But then, a few centuries ago, religious leaders and people couldn't go along with the evidence that Earth is not the center of the universe. A few centuries from now, who knows, God's existence or nonexistence may be more clearly evident for all on Earth and beyond.

As regards to the highly religious spiritual leaders, they have to genuinely work hard all their life to earn this high place status among the believers, who almost worship them even long after they have been laid to rest in their beautifully decorated graves or shrines. One such highly regarded leader, however, once humorously shared his story in confidence with a close friend by telling his secret of how he got there.

He said, "a long time ago I was travelling with hundreds of people in a big boat that got caught in a huge storm of very high magnitude. People were extremely worried and panicky all over the boat, but I sat in a corner as calmly as I could, telling people not to panic because the boat is not going to sink. It so happens that the boat and all of us somehow survived that ordeal but, as a result of my prediction, I was proclaimed a hero with godly powers." He continued, "the prediction was an absolute fake but a smart move on my part. I said to myself that if the boat sinks we will all go with it and the chances are that there will be no survival to question or kick me, but what if the boat and the people survive?"

Now, let's briefly talk about two specific scandals in these religious high places. The first one involves *"religious men sexually abusing minors and nuns"* that has been exploited by the news media in recent months. Besides minors, a 1996 survey recently obtained by a St. Louis newspaper reports that 40% of nuns have also been victims of this scandal or harassment and suffered trauma of some sort.

Without going into any details, the root cause of it has something to do with a religious order that forbids marriage for certain very religious men. This, to a layman like myself, appears to be something against the laws of nature and bio-logical-physiological needs. If we were to continue ignoring that reality, I am afraid that this scandal may and perhaps will continue.

The other shameful episode or scandal is *personal financial gains* by those supposedly managing and administering these high religious institutions. It is of great concern to the religiously faithful many who give a lot of money to these high places with an expectation and blind faith that it would be used for the right purpose.

It appears, however, that only a certain portion or fraction of the total monetary contributions is utilized for the right purpose in some of these places. The local and foreign financial aid providers should make a note of that. The rest of it, you guessed it right, appears to be going into *someone's pocket or personal account.*

When questioned, one of those people with a sense of humor said: I toss up all the money collection from the bowl in the air and say loudly, please God take whatever you need and the rest is mine. Then I pick up all the remaining money off the floor.

These unhealthy situations are partly due to some mismanagement, a universal problem, but mainly because of some personal greed and financial gains and are, therefore, disturbing issues for many. All the auditing once a year of money hoarders' financial situations before and after they took office will barely solve the problem. I say that because a dishonest person can and will invent ways to appear clean during the auditing exercise.

Unfortunately, we may not be able to totally eliminate all the corruption or scandals in these high places. However, in the case of personal financial gains for example, we can eliminate it by having a simple and workable constitution.

A constitution that among other items encourages participation, openness, and effective communication, as well as demands a periodic publication of the financial details or summary. It should also allow ad hoc audit sessions more than just once a year. Furthermore, the constitution should give all members a chance to replace most if not all the current officials every year or two by electing new people who possess positive attitude, are trustworthy, and team players with commitment, dedication, and honesty.

Above all, among those elected, there must be a good leader and mentor who already has or can earn the respect of most if not all; someone who can truly lead and keep the team working together as a team. That someone should be able to motivate people by challenging them and by setting high standards. The leader should be able to use assertive persuasion when needed, delegate with close control, be a good listener, and always have a plan-B ready, just in case.

In addition, a leader who is a good public speaker, can calmly and gracefully handle all the ups and downs of the religious high places, and should also be able to manage human idiosyncrasies or the people factor (see Exhibit-B), which are the most difficult challenges to handle. Remember that this scenario here, like our life's ups and downs, is far from a smooth or straight line.

As religious leaders and organizers or managers of religious high places or institutions, we need to change our attitudes and ethics; the high places' future standing in the world depends on it. If these very practical and proven guidelines are ignored, then the system will sooner or later breakdown and the whole structure will sag of its own weight. More and more people out of frustration will then ask this simple question: Do these corrupt people or money hoarders have no fear of God?

Speaking of God, as an intriguing point once again, Earth as we know is a small part of our Solar System; which is a very small part of our Milky Way Galaxy, which has over 250 billion stars or solar like systems in that one galaxy. As far as the scientists know, there are billions and billions of galaxies in the universe.

This makes Earth to be the most insignificant entity in the big picture of the whole infinite universe. So, why did God choose *Earth* for human beings, which as people believe is "God's greatest creation?"

Treasure Life

___:___:___:___

VIII.

Common Sense

As a Chinese proverb has it: Those who work their minds, rule; those who work their backs are ruled.

So if we were to use our minds and not the blind faith (relating to our backs to be ruled) then we will find that religious guidelines are mostly based on some common sense. Let's use it. Listen to those who say that they have finally found a book, a glorious book that puts it all together for them. Try reading it among others to judge it for yourself. For those who cannot read, ask someone who can read it to you in the language you understand.

At the very least, let's also wish well for fellow human beings and put greater emphasis on doing good deeds toward fellow human beings than on worshipping God. This one universal golden rule applies to the people of all religions. Once we have begun to try to achieve this goal in the true sense, then and only then God will accept you as His worshipper.

For the most part then, let's approach the Almighty as an individual on a daily or on an as frequently as possible basis. Well, because we are born alone, and we will die alone, then why not do this and a few other good things alone as well during our brief stay on Earth?

We certainly don't need a group or anyone else, however more educated or knowledgeable, as an interpreter when trying to approach the Almighty. While we should have the utmost respect for those with greater knowledge and education, we should not be intimidated by them in any way, shape, or form. They have no more or less direct approach to the Almighty than any other individual. Individual or group setting in this context, therefore, may be an issue for those who obviously need help.

For Dr. W. Richard Bond, a scholar and very knowledgeable about several religions first hand, this is a non-issue. He points out, however, that the group settings have certain purpose and advantages such as creating social structures, networks, and marriages.

People's religious extremism quite honestly is an upsetting factor for many. They usually try and avoid associating themselves too closely with the people of extreme views or with any one particular religion openly. To avoid any useless or deaf-ears type of discussion, they simply tell them that we are not very religious people. I can easily relate to all that myself.

However, because of the love of my lovely family, particularly my wife (a loving and caring person, and a devout orator—zakira), and of my rich cultural background full of great poetic literature, I, as an individual, do attend some of the religious or cultural gatherings. I have enjoyed my experiences, particularly, in the places where extremism was not welcomed.

Whether it is for listening to some good local or global poets and orators, or for reciting some of the great poets' work myself with lyrics as part of my culture and background, or as a believer, that really is my own business as an individual. I personally believe that, *for the most part,* my religious business, particularly about approach the Almighty should absolutely be an individual and a private matter; something only between myself and that Almighty, somewhere up there.

To repeat, let's use some common sense, because we, as individuals, certainly don't need a group, mullah, priest, or pundit as interpreters.

Let's now share another point on the subject of common sense. People often say to me "but it's true" because they heard someone say that or they read it somewhere. My first question to them usually is who said it or who wrote it? While we should certainly listen to people and read what someone has written on a subject that interests us, we should always keep in mind that we don't necessarily have to believe in everything we hear or read.

This is due to the fact that most of us tell stories based on our biases, likes, and dislikes. For example, try and listen to the radio or TV stations of two different countries at war with each other. You will most probably get two different accounts or even two opposite stories of the same incident.

So, the only way to get to the truth is to further investigate, if it is important enough for you, or simply use your own judgment and, yes, use common sense. Better still, we should have a mind that is open to everything and attached to nothing.

As part and parcel of common sense, we will have to have the wisdom to distinguish between unrealistic and realistic goals.

For example, it would be unrealistic to expect accomplishing the cardinal-eight *simple ways* for a peaceful world overnight or even in our lifetime. Because it will be a long-term struggle and it may take several decades or perhaps a century to get there, when there will be all new people. As one other example, it would be unrealistic to expect people to practice all religions or to convert all of us to one religion. It's simply not very practical, nor is it possible.

Besides, people will put up roadblocks mainly due to the fact that practically all of us are totally conditioned by identified social structures from the day we are born. It is almost impossible to even minutely change our way of life and our blind faith without an extraordinary, purposeful, and goal directed plan.

Closer to reality, as I see it, is the acceptance and respect of the principle of *different realities,* specifically different people, religions, and cultures—the mother of all realities. We should realize that the people-made differences among religions are every bit as extensive as the differences among many cultures around the world.

Furthermore, don't be afraid to make decisions. We must begin *making decision*s to come up with a strategic plan, test it, and then follow it. For example, we need decisions on religious, political, and other issues like education and poverty. Stop analyzing (ready-aim-aim-aim forever and never shoot) and start experiencing (ready-aim-fire-aim-fire), because when you fire and miss the target, you learn something from it to aim better the next time around.

A final note, once in a while the proud leaders announce some special rebate (e.g., income tax or hydro refund) amounting to let's say $100 each person or household. While people do appreciate receiving it, the amount is hardly noticed by anyone. If we were to multiply that amount by 100 million people in the U.S. alone, it will be equal to $10 billion dollars.

So, here is a common sense question. Wouldn't it be better to utilize that $10 billion dollars for something more creative and worthwhile toward let's say creating a landmark (for example, for the poor, the needy, or the suffering children) that may be appreciatively used for generations?

This may be a change that leaders should introduce by convincing people to willingly say yes. As for the people in general, we must also *accept change* to get energized and not paralyzed. As well, a concerted effort to change will be required, not so much to win rewards but as a way of life.

Finally, stop putting up any roadblocks or blaming your circumstances. Make a real effort to be someone who either makes things happen or watches things happen to learn from them. But certainly don't be one who asks, what happened? All these, once again, are part and parcel of using our common sense. I urge you to use it.

Treasure Life

___:___:___:___

IX.

Conclusion

As with the nature of human notions, the nature of the *abuse of others* discussion in this book suggests drastic changes at the very least in perspective over time. Whether pessimism is the dominant attitude toward other people is impossible to say due to the lack of hard research on the subject. Still, it is difficult to avoid the impression that there is quite widespread resentment of the alleged *people and power* abuses and lack of responsiveness of the faceless tyrants and madmen that appear to many of us to be accountable to no one.

Consciously or unconsciously, we view all the difficult challenges (including human or people idiosyncrasies, illiteracy, and poverty) on the basis of generalized attitudes we possess which in turn are based on broad assumptions. These assumptions cannot be proved in one sense, but they are very real and important in my assessment of any aspect of *the abuse of others*.

It is not being suggested here that people are always consistent in their attitudes and actions, either as individuals or as members of groups. In fact, the opposite is probably closer to the truth since as individuals we can very easily, if unknowingly, be quite inconsistent in our views.

The problem for many seems to be that they are uncertain about whom to blame for these difficult challenges or conditions, which they, as individuals or as groups, define as problems in our society. That is, a situation may be agreed upon as a problem by a great number of people who cannot agree among themselves on the direction in which the finger of blame ought to point.

Some appear to lay the cause of most if not all ills on the ineptness and blindness of the politicians and religious leaders, whereas others stress the greed of the *people and power* abusers. Yet another group suspects the lobbying, brainwashing, and bribing the superpower leaders by a wealthy minority with ulterior motives are the root causes; this tiny but influential minority, as some believe, constantly and skillfully uses the superpower leaders as pawns, hence, for all intents and purposes, rules the world.

In this text, however, I have attempted to leave my particular biases aside to neutrally present and assess the factual information as well as the controversies relevant to various topic areas, although I must admit that complete lack of bias is quite impossible.

Some questions remain at the heart of the problematical nature of *the abuse of others*, a calamity which, I feel, is quite unlikely to change in the foreseeable future. The reader must, therefore, personally attempt to sort out what appears to be the reality and what ought to be the reality of the world we live in.

Finally, knowledge is power to the extent to which one is either interested in or concerned about all the ills in the world. Pursuit of such knowledge or truth, as difficult as it may seem, must be regarded as essential for succeeding in the creation of a peaceful world. As for the truth, let's revisit *The Life Model* (see Exhibit-A) that urges people to crave for the truth and spread it among the people of the world.

More specifically, it's worth repeating what I wrote at the beginning of my humble composition. Imagine, just for a moment, that you are not a Buddhist, Christian, Hindu, Jew, or Muslim, but, instead, would like to become a great *human being to make life meaningful*, the teachings of all major religions. If we were to achieve a fraction of this goal in the true sense, then we would begin the *acceptance of and respect for different people, religions, and cultures,* and also commence the glorious journey toward developing a passion for people to gain *inner and lasting peace.*

This naturally would also help raise the level of compassion we have for our own religious beliefs as a truly good Buddhist (e.g., Theravada, Mahayana), Christian (e.g., Catholic, Protestant), Hindu (e.g., Brahman, Kshatriya), Jew (e.g., Orthodox, Reform), and Muslim (e.g., Sunni, Shi'a). And that, I am sure, would make this world a better place to live for all of us.

I encourage the people of the world to deeply consider and respect the fact that we are all very different. I urge more and more people to crave for the truth and become *great human beings* through the *acceptance* and *respect* of *different people, cultures, and religions—the mother of all realities.*

Nothing less than achieving excellence in determination and conviction to succeed in creating a peaceful world would be needed to handle the most difficult *challenge* of all, human idiosyncrasies, or the people factor (see Exhibit-B).

The strength of the *just people power,* the biggest power of all, will be needed to remove the *people and power* abusers known as the madmen, the religious gurus with extreme or destructive views, and the tyrant political superpower-lords. They have made many people lose touch with the magic and beauty of religion and life.

A twenty-twenty vision will be required to eradicate illiteracy and poverty, the root causes of all the troubles and problems in the world today, by promoting education, which undoubtedly is one of the most essential ingredients for our success in creating a peaceful world.

Another very pressing challenge is the abuse of the name of religion with many bloody confrontations and conflicts among four of the world's major religions—Judaism, Islam, Hinduism, and Christianity. These conflicts, as detailed in Chapter—I are: the unfortunate 9/11 September 11, 2001 attacks on the U.S.A. with political connotations, and the decades old continuing struggles in Kashmir (the East), Northern Ireland (the West), and the Middle East (particularly, Palestine).

If we, the people who believe in right and just cause, don't wake-up to stop further bloodshed and suffering in the name of religion, power, politics, or whatever else, it may destroy the axis of our thousands-of-years-old civilization and with it, humankind. Because of the sheer frustration of not winning any wars combined with the fear of the inevitable downfall of its powerful era, the nation that already has such experience may start a nuclear war.

We must therefore persistently and assertively persuade all the powers directly or indirectly involved to tackle these conflicts and challenges by getting to the root causes of *the abuse of others* instead.

The just people must demand a sincere, impartial, and concerted effort by using nonviolent and peaceful means, to make people learn to live as good neighbors. Make people respect each other's religious beliefs and understand the human right to exist with dignity in their own homes.

A sincere effort by all to move toward creating a lasting peace will virtually eliminate human suffering and current huge military expenditure. This means saving human lives and enormous savings in monetary terms. We can then utilize a fraction of these savings to fight much bigger wars of *eliminating religious and political tension* **and** *illiteracy and poverty* around the world.

Let's make a real effort to succeed in: changing attitude, people, and systems; eliminating scandals, extremism, criticism, and major political and religious conflicts; and *putting greater emphasis on doing good deeds toward fellow human beings than on worshipping God*. That, in the final analysis, and believing in the shared ancestry of *Abraham*, a model of sacrifice for three major religions, are the keys to begin a glorious journey toward developing a passion for people to *make life meaningful.*

To gain *inner and lasting peace*, we must also learn from the grand Models of Life and Models for Right vs. Wrong. The magnificent seven, as I call them, are, Moses of the Land of Israel, The Buddha of the Himalayas, Jesus Christ of Nazareth, Imam Hussain b. Ali of Arabia, Mahatma Gandhi of the Indian Subcontinent, Mao Tse Tung of China, and John F. Kennedy of the United States of America.

Clearly then, and only then, the love we feel for people, the respect we have for other religions and cultures, and the level of compassion we have for our own religion's uniqueness will increase dramatically for our ultimate goal of treasuring life.

We can do it by working together as cohesive teams of strong coalitions worldwide and by using the strength of alliances among the just to achieve our just goal of creating a peaceful world without any superficial and unnatural international borders.

We can also raise our self-esteem to great heights, as Dr. M. Iqbal—the Persian, Urdu, and English languages poet-philosopher of the twentieth century from the Indo-Pakistan Subcontinent—wrote, and I am making an attempt here to translate it:

Raise the self-esteem to such great heights that,
before every destiny,

> *God Himself asks His human being,*
> *say what's your wish.* _____

Our only wish is *to evolve a peaceful world* by using peaceful means for making life more meaningful.

Finally, we should not and cannot force or push people to work toward creating a peaceful world through some overnight revolutions, because it is going to be a mammoth task for all the peoples of the world to achieve it through a pull methodology and an evolutionary process over decades. Remember that a push methodology on people usually gets the opposite result.

However, we have to passionately try to accomplish it all with high level of determination and deep conviction. In doing so, the hope will prevail through the strength of the just people power, and so will its potential that can be realized.

Let's not wait until the muck reaches our eyes through wars, conflicts, suppression, hate, and violence. My hope is that more and more people will be inspired by other people's giant step toward achieving peace alongside my own humble and tiny effort here in this book, to cope with the unparalleled challenges ahead. Let's begin by trying to convince superpower-lords and others that earning a place in history for true heroism means making peace not wars.

Much more needs to be said for stopping *the abuse of others* calamity. For now, however, that will be all. I hope that the guidelines, framework, or near strategies in this book have been, and will continue to be, helpful to all the people of the world. Let's not forget the most basic strategy of all, ***we can do it***. My sincere best wishes will always be with you all.

Let's now end here by repeating—a thousand times every year, that means about three times a day—something I wrote earlier.

When all the aforementioned essential ingredients for success in creating a peaceful world have been attained in the true sense, let's hope and pray that our book's title *So Close, Yet So Far Apart—Stopping the Abuse of Others*—will become a thing of the past. Amen.

Shalom, Salaam, Namaskar,…Peace!

Treasure Life

____:____:____:____

Syed H. Jaffar
sjaffar@idirect.com

0-595-32632-3